WHY THE CHURCH WILL NOT GO THROUGH THE TRIBULATION

Copyright © 1982
by The Southwest Radio Church

All rights reserved including the right of
reproduction in whole or in part in any form.

Published by

SOUTHWEST RADIO CHURCH
P.O. Box 1144
Oklahoma City, Oklahoma 73101

1 copy for $5.00 offering; 3 copies for $10.00
offering; $1.50 each in lots of 25 or more.

TABLE OF CONTENTS

1. ISRAEL AND THE CHURCH 1
2. GOD'S COVENANT WITH ISRAEL 8
3. THE BLESSED HOPE 13
4. PRE — MID — POST — ? 19
5. FALSE CHRISTS 24
6. OLD TESTAMENT MODELS 28
7. THE SEVEN FEASTS OF ISRAEL 32
8. REVELATION OF JESUS CHRIST 37

Chapter One
ISRAEL AND THE CHURCH

DR. GAVERLUK: Rob Lindsted, Ph.D., former professor of engineering at Wichita University, is now giving his life completely to witnessing for the Lord along with holding science and Bible conferences across the country. I want to ask you a question which is paramount in the hearts and minds of the vast majority of people who are doing any thinking about what is happening today. The question is: Is the world going to be destroyed by men?

DR. LINDSTED: Well, while looking at current events and at the news each night, one would almost have a sick feeling in his stomach because there is so much bad news. But as you read the Bible you see that there are two groups of people who have a hope.

DR. GAVERLUK: What are these two groups?

DR. LINDSTED: The two groups that biblically have a hope are: (1) the church and (2) Israel.

DR. GAVERLUK: Let's start with Israel. Why are the Jews so important?

DR. LINDSTED: There are two main reasons why Israel is important. As you go to the Word of God, you find that God has made promises to Israel for the future. You find in much of the Old Testament that God reveals His person through His dealings with the nation of Israel. Israel began with Abraham, Abraham's descendants and Abraham's children. For a long time it looked as though there was no hope for Israel but eventually a 99 year-old man and his 99 year-old wife had a son. That son became the forefather of the nation of Israel.

Israel and her history is portrayed in the Old Testament. As we come to the New Testament we find that there is a scattering of Israel. Of course Israel was reborn in May 1948. So even though for over 1800 years there was no nation of Israel, from A.D. 70 until 1948, now Israel is very much back in the focus of the news, very much back in the focus of those who are looking for the plan of God to take its course.

DR. GAVERLUK: Where is this special promise to Israel in the Old Testament?

DR. LINDSTED: The original promise is found in Genesis 12:1-3. However, it is interesting that this promise is renewed and repeated time after time.

DR. GAVERLUK: Let's read Genesis 12:2,13: *"I will make of thee a great nation, and I will bless thee, and make thy name great; and thou shalt be a blessing: And I will bless them that bless thee, and curse him that curseth thee: and in thee shall all families of the earth be blessed."*

DR. LINDSTED: You can see that that promise has not really been fulfilled to its complete expectation.

DR. GAVERLUK: What does it mean? Does it mean that Israel is going to become the greatest nation on earth at some time?

DR. LINDSTED: Yes, I believe that the Bible is clear that through the blessings of God Israel will become the dominant nation of Earth.

DR. GAVERLUK: When is that going to be? Certainly it hasn't happened in the last 2,000 years.

DR. LINDSTED: No, it hasn't happened in the last 2,000 years because for most of those 2,000 years, Israel was not a nation. Only in the last 34 years have they again become a nation.

DR. GAVERLUK: That in itself is a miracle.

DR. LINDSTED: It sure is. As a matter of fact, Israel was born in a miracle. That is when this baby named Isaac was born to a 99 year-old man and a 99 year-old woman. That was a miracle; a miracle birth for the first seed in Israel. Now we're looking at another miracle. Israel was born as a nation in May 1948 and so for 1,870 years there was no nation of Israel. Now there is a nation of Israel and now God can begin to fulfill the great promises that He made — that they will be a great nation. I think that's talking about the kingdom age that is yet to come.

Next, God said He will bless them because he will give them a great name. Their name is not great. In other words, while they do make the news, people are not thrilled with the name of Israel. God continued to say that He will *"curse those who curse thee . . . "* And as well, every family will be blessed as a result of the nation of Israel.

DR. GAVERLUK: That one phrase *". . . curse him that curseth thee . . . "* seems to have wide application. I can't help but feel that somehow the downfall of the British Empire had something to do with the fact that they didn't treat the Jews right.

DR. LINDSTED: I think that is exactly right. One of the prayers that we should have in this country is that we continue to respect the nation of Israel and continue to give honor to it because the nation is God's earthly people.

DR. GAVERLUK: Doesn't that tie in with what Jesus said about any who mistreated His brethren, and of course His brethren are the Jews. Jesus was a Jew. If we treat them right God will reward us. If not, then the curse that is found in Genesis 12 will affect us just as much as it will or has affected every other nation. As a matter of fact, you can look at all the nations that have mistreated the Jews and see the suffering and trouble that they have received as a result.

DR. LINDSTED: Yes, that is right. We think especially of Germany in recent history. Consider the Russian persecution that is going on right now. Russia is not prospering, and will not simply because God's Word has made it very clear that Israel is one of the two groups that has hope from God.

DR. GAVERLUK: Do you believe that this is actually the criteria (how they treated the Jews) by which nations will be allowed into the Millennium, the kingdom that Jesus is going to establish?

DR. LINDSTED: Yes, I do. Matthew 25, where it deals with the judgment of the nations, appears to be directly related to their treatment of the nation of Israel.

DR. GAVERLUK: So in effect as we watch our own government and their reaction to this invasion by Israel of Lebanon, and what we are going to do about all of this, means that we are walking a very tight rope here!

DR. LINDSTED: That is right. I think it is also important to point out that that does not mean that we agree with Israel every time Israel does something, but it means that our friendship is stronger than any one circumstance, any one event. So we should continue to pray that our government might be sensitive to Israel.

DR. GAVERLUK: Of course Israel still has to go through the Tribulation period, and that means that Israel will be judged for her actions.

DR. LINDSTED: That's right. Israel is not finished. The work that God has to do through Israel has just begun. Israel will have to go through a refining time.

DR. GAVERLUK: Are you going to be talking about the purposes of Israel's going through the Tribulation?

DR. LINDSTED: Yes, I am. I really think the key to understanding the Tribulation, is knowing what it is about. God does not allow a period of time like the Tribulation without having a purpose for it. There is a definite purpose for the Tribulation, and it is related to Israel and God's plan for Israel.

DR. GAVERLUK: Would you say God wills the Tribulation or He allows the Tribulation? Would you say He allows sin to come to a head?

DR. LINDSTED: I believe that according to God's law and God's Word, Israel has to go through the Tribulation in order for it to be refined. It doesn't bring pleasure to the heart of God to persecute Israel the way they will be persecuted, but He knows that in the end time, Israel will be refined, beautiful and will recognize God for who He is. He knows it will be worth it even though it will be a terrible time of trouble.

DR. GAVERLUK: So all the promises that God gave Israel in the Old Testament will ultimately be fulfilled.

DR. LINDSTED: That is right. II Corinthians 1:20 says: *"Every promise of God . . . . is yea . . . and Amen . . . . "* In other words every promise of God will be fulfilled; it is guaranteed. That is a great hope that we have.

DR. GAVERLUK: Will you define the Church?

DR. LINDSTED: The Church is those people who have received by faith Jesus Christ as their Savior. The Church began on the Day of Pentecost, and all who were believers were brought into one body, one group.

DR. GAVERLUK: Now this means that any person — regardless of what nationality, regardless of the color of his skin — has an equal opportunity to believe that Jesus Christ is God, that Jesus Christ did die for him, and put his trust solely in Christ. The believer then has the assurance of eternal life.

DR. LINDSTED: That is right. Jesus Christ makes them one body. Christ is one Head, so there is one body. If we had only one head and two bodies, we would have a monstrosity. Or if we had one body and several heads, we would also have a monstrosity. Now, the Church is the other group that has a hope for the future.

DR. GAVERLUK: It must have been a shock to Israel to realize that she was not the only chosen group.

DR. LINDSTED: Yes, I am sure that it was. As a matter of fact it was discussed by the apostles in Acts 15. Remember at what we call the Council of Jerusalem, the apostles were discussing this and after the discussion they summarized it saying: *"And after they had held their peace, James answered, saying, Men and brethren, hearken unto me: Simeon hath declared how God at the first did visit the Gentiles, to take out of them a people for his name. And to this agree the words of the prophets; as it is written, After this I will return, and will build again the tabernacle of David, which is fallen down; and I will build it again the ruins thereof, and I will set it up . . . "* (Acts 15:13-16).

Here the early apostles recognized that God was going to deal with both the Church and with Israel, but His dealings with Israel would come after He called out people from all nations. And that is exactly what He was doing. The conclusion of the Council of Jerusalem in Acts 15 was this: Gentiles can be saved and can be included into this one body. This body is called the Church.

DR. GAVERLUK: The word "church" is from the Greek "ekklesia." What does it mean?

DR. LINDSTED: It means a called out assembly, or group of people.

DR. GAVERLUK: But we're not talking about an organization?

DR. LINDSTED: Oh, no!

DR. GAVERLUK: We are talking about a living organism. This is also symbolized in the New Testament as being the Body of Christ and the Bride of Christ. What do those two terms mean?

DR. LINDSTED: I think there are two things interesting about those two analogies. The Body of Christ is an interesting way to put it because He is Lord over creation. He is not a part of creation. When we are in the body of Christ, He actually links Himself together with those who have believed in Him. That is a very special way for the Creator, the Savior, to be linked with us. It is vastly different than creation. He is Lord over creation. But while He is the Head over the Church, we are a part of Him. We are the body and He is the Head.

Now the Bride of Christ refers especially to the hope we have that when Christ comes back, He will claim His Bride and we are His Bride! The Bride shows the special affection that Christ has for the Church, and the body shows our special relationship that we have to Christ as the Head.

DR. GAVERLUK: There is a wonderful book entitled *Destined For The Throne.* I was startled when I read the statement: *". . . that the whole universe, that the planet earth, the whole human race, all history were for one purpose: God purposed to bring forth a Bride to rule and reign with His Son, the Lord Jesus."*

DR. LINDSTED: That is really the purpose of the Bible, to show how we can be part of the Bride. Christ did not come looking for a servant or a slave, He came wooing a Bride, and that is the Church.

DR. GAVERLUK: Israel is not going to be left out.

DR. LINDSTED: No, but it is important to see that while there are these two groups that have a hope (Israel and the Church), they are not necessarily the same. In other words there are Jewish people who can be saved during the church age and become part of this body, or a part of the Chruch. Even though they both have a hope, God deals in contrasting ways with the Church and with the nation of Israel.

DR. GAVERLUK: The Church is actually to be taken out of the world where Israel is going to be brought into the world and into a vital new relationship during the Millennium. This is the only nation in the world that has this promise!

Now let's go back to the Old Testament. As I said before, Israel was in a state of shock at the sudden disappearance of (I'm making a guess here) 300 million living people on Earth. They suddenly disappear and nobody knows where they are, they can't find a single trace. They can't find a single body, dead or alive, that belongs to the Church, that belongs to Christ. Israel expresses this shock in Psalm 12:1: *"Help, Lord;* (save Lord) *for the godly man ceaseth . . . "* The word "ceaseth" is similar to the word "gamar," which means the godly are fulfilled, the godly are completed. This implies: look at us we aren't fulfilled, we aren't completed.Your promises have not been totally fulfilled for us. It then goes on: *". . . for the faithful fail from among the children of men."* The word fail is "pacac" meaning to vanish. The faithful have vanished, and we are left alone. Israel is crying out in anguish here in Psalm 12:1.

When I look at Micah 7:1, there is the same idea: *"Woe is me!* (Israel is saying) *for I am as when they have gathered the summer fruits, as the grape gleanings of the vintage: there is no cluster to eat: my soul desired the firstripe fruit."* They thought they were going to get the firstripe fruit, but they didn't get it. God did something else. When Israel delayed in her repentance to the Lord, the Lord just went right out into the world and picked Himself a great group of people. When they are removed, He takes up the cause of Israel again. Obviously that is what He is doing right now. This is a very exciting time in which to be living.

DR. LINDSTED: The words in Acts 15 verify that very thought becuase it says: *"After this . . . . "* In other words, He will first deal with the Church. When He is through dealing with the Church, he will then come and begin to deal again expressly with the nation of Israel. His dealings with the Church on Earth will then be complete. I think it is the hope of every Christian, every believer in Christ, that Jesus Christ will return soon.

DR. GAVERLUK: Now with that, all the events start to take place. That means that God takes up the cause of Israel, and Israel is to be saved out of this world crisis that is coming. It is quite a story as revealed in the Old Testament!

DR. LINDSTED: Yes, it is. It is interesting that we are already referring to the fact that there is a surprise "taking-out" of the Church. Now sometimes people are hesitant to use that phrase "surprise taking-out." It is interesting to see that in contrast to Israel, the hope that the Church has is the sudden appearing of Christ, a surprise appearing of Christ; whereas Israel will begin to see the hand of God, working day by day as He deals with them during this Tribulation, and they will come back to God. But for the Church, they already recognize God for who He is. They already recognize Christ for the fact that He is the Savior. It will be a surprise taking out or a sudden snatching away. This is referred to as the "rapture" of the church.

DR. GAVERLUK: We're talking about the fact that God is getting ready to close the books on the Church and open the books on Israel. I think that is a very apt statement to be made today. Perhaps that explains the tremendous and amazing thing that has happened in regard to Israel in recent wars and in the deliverance of her people. For example note the rescue at Entebbe and her successful raid on the Baghdad nuclear installation. Obviously Daniel's expression of the angel, the guardian angel of Israel is really working!

DR. LINDSTED: Yes, God has certainly protected Israel! He has intervened for Israel in a miraculous way! I believe that just as He has allowed the Church to see examples of Israel in the Old Testament so that we might walk well from their past examples, He is now allowing the Church to see how He is dealing with Israel in a miraculous way so we might refine our walk even by looking at current events as they fulfill Bible prophecy.

DR. GAVERLUK: When you walk the streets of Jerusalem while visiting Israel, you sense that these people seem to realize that they have a destiny, and that is why they are there.

DR. LINDSTED: Yes, that is what really marks Israel as being different from every other nation. They have a hope of Messiah's coming. They have a hope given to them in the Old Testament. They indeed will be a nation to reckon with on this Earth. That is why, even in spite of insurmountable odds, they are willing to go into battles and are willing to do things that other nations would say are too risky. They believe their God-given hope as recorded in the Old Testament.

DR. GAVERLUK: It is astounding to watch what is taking place. One incredible instance that occurred was when they drove their tanks into the Sinai desert and didn't know where the mine fields were, a sudden, great wind came up, blew the sand away and revealed the tops of the mines. There are many other instances like this which show that God is obviously doing something with Israel and will protect the real Israel, the spiritual Israel, the remnant of Israel during the time of the Tribulation. The time of the Tribulation is known as the time of Jacob's trouble (Jeremiah 30:7). What does that mean?

DR. LINDSTED: I believe it means God is going to use the Tribulation as a special time to awaken Israel to the real plan in God's whole prophetic scheme. And so, He describes it as the time of Jacob's trouble so we won't be confused, thinking this is the time when the Church will be purified. The Church is to be purified by the hope of His coming. Israel will be purified as they go through this Tribulation period. That is why He refers to it as Jacob's trouble.

DR. GAVERLUK: That is very well put! I'm looking at Isaiah 63 which tells of the confrontation of Israel, the remnant Israel, with her Messiah. The conversation is actually recorded in Isaiah 63: 1-4: *"Who is this that cometh from Edom, with dyed garments from Bozrah? . . . this that is glorious in his apparel, travelling in the greatness of his strength?"* And He replies: *"I that speak in righteousness, mighty to save."* And then she says: *"Wherefore art thou red in thine apparel, and thy garments like him that treadeth in the winefat?"* And He says: *"I have trodden the winepress alone; and of the people there was none with me: for I will tread them in mine anger, and trample them in my fury; and their blood shall be sprinkled upon my garments, and I will stain all my raiment. For the day of vengeance is in mine heart, and the year of my redeemed is come."*

DR. LINDSTED: You know, it is beautiful to see how God offers hope to both the Church and Israel, and how different their hope really is! For Israel, their hope comes as they go through this Tribulation, this time of God's testing on them and on the whole world. For the Church, our hope comes when Christ reappears.

DR. GAVERLUK: I am wondering about Isaiah 63:1. Here is a point of confrontation. They will be in Petra at this time. Now the question is, how will Christ get there and what will happen? He leads them back to Jerusalem from Petra. We find that in Isaiah 35:10, it says: *"And the ransomed of the Lord shall return, and come to Zion with songs and everlasting joy upon their heads: they shall obtain joy and gladness, and sorrow and sighing shall flee away."* And that will be the beginning of the Millennium for them. What a marvelous hope they have!

To those who are reading this, please recognize that we are talking about events that are taking place today. We are living at the climax of history, and you want to be prepared for the coming of the Lord Jesus Christ. I hope and pray that He is your Lord and your Savior, so that you can eagerly look forward to that moment when you will meet the Lord in the air.

Chapter Two
GOD'S COVENANT WITH ISRAEL

DR. GAVERLUK: What we are doing now is contrasting God's program for Israel with His program for the Church. We defined Israel and the Church in our first chapter, and we now want to present a brief outline of the climax of Israel's history as she moves from the present phase of her existence into a wonderful new phase that God has promised for thousands of years. We are about to see that being accomplished. Israel is expecting her Messiah, and her Messiah is going to come to her in Petra. We get that from Psalm 60:9: *"Who will bring me into the strong city?* (This is Israel speaking.) *who will lead me into Edom?"* And that, of course, means that Petra, in Edom will be the place where the remnant of Israel will have a haven of safety for three and one-half years. Messiah will not come to Israel in the Palestinian area, but rather to Petra to meet the remnant.

Next we look at Isaiah 63:1: *"Who is this that cometh from Edom . . . from Bozrah?"* Bozrah was the ancient capital of Edom and it is just north of Petra. So obviously the Messiah is coming from Jerusalem, and He is covered with blood as that chapter shows. That means that He has been at Armageddon. He has taken care of the nations that have surrounded Jerusalem and He has destroyed them. Now He comes for His people. His people will have been in Petra for three and one-half years waiting for the Messiah to come. He is going to lead them back to Jerusalem as prophesied in Psalm 35:10.

If the Tribulation were to begin this year, that event would be at least seven years away. It is evidently going to be a little bit longer than that, but you do believe that is going to occur very soon?

DR. LINDSTED: Yes, I do. I think every current event points to the soon return of Christ. Every Bible promise and prophecy points to the soon return of Christ. I am looking for Christ to come; to steal or snatch away the Church, and then to begin His work with Israel that will prepare them for exactly this point in time.

DR. GAVERLUK: Revelation 12:6,14, indicates that Israel is the woman that flees to the wilderness where God will feed her for three and one-half years and take care of her. (One-third of the Jews in the land of Israel at the time the Great Tribulation begins will be saved — Zechariah 13:8,9. Based on the present population of Israel, that would be a little over one million.)

DR. LINDSTED: When you realize that God took care of several million Israelites in the wilderness for forty years, He surely isn't going to have trouble taking care of the Jewish remnant in Petra for three and one-half years!

DR. GAVERLUK: But this is a modern day! We have rockets that we can deliver from one side of the earth over to the other side. It appears there would be no place to hide at all, and yet here is a nation that will be preserved through the Tribulation period, while all the other nations suffer from the judgments prophesied in the Book of Revelation. I am reminded of something that happened during the Second World War. One-hundred thousand British soldiers were backed up against the English Channel at Dunkirk. Hitler thought he had them and the German airforce was ready to destroy them. Suddenly a great fog came over that whole area, a fog so thick they could hardly see their hands in front of their faces. The English Channel, which is normally very choppy and tricky, became as a sea of glass. What happened was that from England boats went out — large boats and small boats — all the way across and they rescued 100,000 soldiers and brought them back to Great Britain. That in itself was a vast miracle. So that is a demonstration of how God can hide Israel in Petra. Israel will be protected in this place. I was there and visited it. It is an amazing place. The only way to get into it is through The Siq. It is about a mile long, a little wider than a jeep with cliffs which go up to 500 feet high. Suddenly you see the treasury building, which is cut right out of the cliff. Here Israel will be kept safe for three and one-half years at a time when Armageddon will be raging on Earth. This is the promise of Scripture.

What we have drawn now is a contrast in the way God is going to deliver Israel. Now we come to the question, how is God going to deliver the Church? The Church is evidently not going to be here on Earth simultaneously.

DR. LINDSTED: That is right. I think this is where we really need to see that God has two plans: one for Israel and one for the Church. We have been discussing how God would preserve Israel, but His plan for the Church is different. He plans to call them out (to catch or take them out). This is the rapture.

DR. GAVERLUK: The word rapture is not in the Bible!

DR. LINDSTED: No, it is not. However, just because the word is not in the Bible does not mean it isn't scriptural.

DR. GAVERLUK: I am going to change my mind here and say that it is in the Bible if you read the Latin Vulgate. So it is a Latin word.

DR. LINDSTED: Yes, it is a Latin word and it simply means, "to snatch up, or to catch away." That is really what God has promised the Church.

DR. GAVERLUK: The Church is to be caught up from planet Earth, up into space, to meet the Lord in the air. That event will not be at the end of the Tribulation period which is the same time Jesus will lead Israel to Jerusalem.

DR. LINDSTED: That is right. When He comes to rapture the Christians, He comes FOR the Christians. As we read in Revelation 19, we see that when He comes for Israel, He will actually come WITH the saints. So the first event is FOR the saints, and the next one is WITH the saints.

DR. GAVERLUK: Actually we are going to be watching Him as He goes to Petra and meets with Israel face to face. Then we are told in Psalm 2:1—4 that at the height of Armageddon: *"Why do the heathen rage, and the people imagine a vain thing? The kings of the earth set themselves, and the rulers take counsel together, against the Lord, and against his anointed, saying, Let us break their bands asunder . . . . He that sitteth in the heavens shall laugh: the Lord shall have them in derision."* When we come to the tenth verse we read: *"Be wise now therefore, O ye kings: be instructed, ye judges of the earth."* That is not ordinary kings from planet Earth. These kings and judges represent the Church. We will come with Christ to judge Israel and the rest of the nations.

DR. LINDSTED: So we really see that there is a striking contrast. This striking contrast is parallel to when Christ came the first time. He came as a babe the first time. He will come as a warrior the second time. He was wrapped in death clothes the first time. When He comes again, He will wear a vesture, war clothes. The first time He came He rode on a colt, the foal of an ass. The second time He comes to Earth, He will come riding on a white horse. He came the first time and was crowned with thorns. The second time He comes He will be crowned with many crowns. So there is a striking contrast between His first coming and His second coming. There is a striking contrast when He comes FOR the Church and when He comes WITH the Church for Israel.

DR. GAVERLUK: I heard a wonderful sermon preached by Dr. Bailey Smith here in Oklahoma. He said that Jesus will be wearing crowns. Who is it that will give those crowns to Him? Dr. Smith said they will be our crowns that we will have given to Him! I almost jumped up with joy in that church, because this is a thrilling thought! We are coming with the Lord. It is wonderful what the Lord has in store for those who love Him and serve Him. He has a very careful plan that He is working out for the Church.

DR. LINDSTED: Yes, He sure does! As we continue to compare the Church and Israel, I think there is a series of points we should make to distinguish how God is carrying out His plan. For example, if we are to look at the hope that Christ gives to the Church, this hope is the fact that He will come FOR them. But if we look at the hope that Israel has, their hope is when Christ comes WITH the saints, not for the saints. In a similar way, when He comes for the Church, this event is a sudden thing. In reading John 14, I Thessalonians 4 and I Corinthians 15, let us examine each passage in this particular series. We see that there are no signs given so that the Church can say, "Ok, we know that tomorrow He is coming." But it is always this, "Today — maybe today Christ will come." When He comes He will snatch away the Church. There is really no mention of anyone seeing Him prior to the rapture. But when He returns for Israel, it will be a public event. All eyes will see Him. Where at the rapture, He comes in the clouds; when He comes at the end of the Tribulation, He will come all the way to Earth.

DR. GAVERLUK: Actually, Israel may know the time simply because of what is stated in the Scripture. When that Abomination of Desolation is set up, they can start counting off the days and they can tell exactly when the Messiah is going to come. We read in Daniel 12:11: *"And from the time that the daily sacrifice shall be taken away, and the abomination that maketh desolate set up, there shall be a thousand two hundred and ninety days. Blessed is he that waiteth, and cometh to the thousand three hundred and five and thirty days."* So actually the timing has been given to Israel. Israel will start counting off from the time that the Antichrist sets up his image in the temple.

DR. LINDSTED: Yes, that is right. Daniel 12 refers to the wise who will know. In other words, once the Church is gone and the Tribulation starts, Israel can know the time sequence.

DR. GAVERLUK: Even though there is no such timetable for the Church, you do believe in the imminent return of Christ.

DR. LINDSTED: Yes, I do. The reason why it is so important to believe in the imminent return of Christ is that it has a profound effect on our life. If we thought that we had to live through part or all of the Tribulation, there would be no incentive to live completely for Christ right now.

DR. GAVERLUK: So instead of looking for Christ, we would be looking for the Tribulation! We would then be taking our eyes off Christ.

DR. LINDSTED: This is exactly the point that the epistle authors were trying to make as they wrote by inspiration of God in the first century. They stressed the importance of expecting the return of Christ. As we begin developing the point that the Church does not go through the Tribulation or through any part of the Tribulation, it is important for us to support our premillennial position with Scripture.

DR. GAVERLUK: When we're referring to the second coming of Christ, we are talking about two phases of the same second coming, not just one. This is only one part of the second coming. We must not allow people to be confused and say: "You teach two second comings."

DR. LINDSTED: Phase one is when He comes in the clouds and takes up the Church (that is the Christians).

DR. GAVERLUK: Now, will all the world see Him at that time?

DR. LINDSTED: No, they won't see Him then, but in phase two He will come with those that He took up earlier (the Church) and He will be seen by everyone. In Revelation 1:7 it says: *". . . every eye will see him . . . ."*

DR. GAVERLUK: Now I know you are going to expound on this, but why is there this difference? There is a time element between the two events but what is the purpose of this time period?

DR. LINDSTED: In one He is dealing with the Church, and in the other He is dealing with Israel. Yes, there is a difference in the time frame. One phase of Christ's return occurs at least seven years later than the other. After He has translated the Church, the Antichrist is then revealed, begins his work and the Tribulation occurs on the Earth. Then Christ returns to rescue Israel from the reign of Antichrist and the judgment that is on the Earth.

DR. GAVERLUK: Could it be that God can't do anything with Israel until the Church disappears because God's witness in the world is still the Church?

DR. LINDSTED: Yes, that's right. I think that He is reserving His full plan for Israel until after the Church is gone. That is the Acts 15 idea "after this." "After this" He will come back and He will begin to deal expressly with Israel.

DR. GAVERLUK: Tell me, do you think all of this is going to happen in this decade? Is it a possibility?

DR. LINDSTED: Well, I believe that Christ's coming is so near that our hope is that Christ will come today. Take note of Matthew 24:48: *". . . that evil servant shall say in his heart, My lord delayeth his coming;"* It implies this: The evil servant says, Christ's coming is delayed one more day. The only proper way for the believer to live is to believe and to live like Christ is coming right now, today. If we say, "I really don't think He's coming until tomorrow," then we are not looking for the Blessed Hope, the soon return of Christ, as we should.

For example, I John 2:18 says: *"Little children, it is the last time: and as ye have heard that antichrist shall come, even now are there many antichrists; whereby we know that it is the last time."* Then the Apostle continued in verse 28: *"And now, little children, abide in him; that, when he shall appear, we may have confidence, and not be ashamed before him at his coming."* In other words, John, one of the writers of the New Testament epistles, looked for the imminent return of Christ. He could say that it is the last time. Don't look for a whole series of signs, but look for the coming of Christ. It is important for us to understand the motive for it as given in I John 3:3: *"And every man that hath this hope in him purifieth himself, even as he is pure."* So I find those that are looking for the imminent return of Christ have a real urgency about how they live the Christian life. This is important. This is the teaching of Christ; this is the teaching of every writer of the New Testament epistles.

DR. GAVERLUK: The question is asked, where would you want to be when Jesus comes? Would you want Him to see where you are? In some bad place? Or in some good place? That is a question that every one of us should ask ourself. Consider Hosea 6:1-2: *"Come, and let us return unto the Lord: for he hath torn, and he will heal us;*(says Israel) *he hath smitten, and he will bind us up."* This is for the remnant of Israel in the Tribulation. When the High Priest has brought Israel to her knees before the Messiah, he says, *"After two days will he revive us . . . "* If we take this literally, it means two days of repentance. The High Priest continues: *". . . in the third day he will raise us up, and we* shall live in his sight." With complete repentance, Jesus will begin His kingdom reign in two days' time.

DR. LINDSTED: Yes, and that is a beautiful model. I use the word model to mean a representation, because the two days also have a reference to the Church Age. For two days Hosea said Israel would lie still. During those two days, or two thousand years, that is the Church Age, God has been calling out of the Gentiles a people for His Name. But in the third day, or the third thousand years, the Kingdom Age which will follow the Tribulation, Israel will receive her promises. And so in Hosea, God's picture book for the nation of Israel, we read that God would call out a Gentile people, a Church, for two days, and one day is as a thousand years. But in the third day, in the third thousand years after they rejected Christ, Israel will be a people to be reckoned with on the earth.

DR. GAVERLUK: Israel will be with the Church, living here and working on a beautiful restored planet, and it is going to be just absolutely marvelous. We as Christians are being prepared for that wonderful moment when we shall hear the Lord's shout from space, the sound of a trumpet, the dead in Christ shall be raised first. Then we which are alive are to be suddenly snatched up to meet the Lord in the air. I have thought about it for years, and I don't think any one of us can fully comprehend the total significance of what is going to happen to us.

DR. LINDSTED: What a tremendous responsibility we have to urge people to be ready. If indeed we are on the verge of the Rapture, people must be ready. They must realize that Christ is the solution, Christ is our salvation. By faith we must accept what Christ did on the Cross, not relying on anything other than the finished work of Jesus Christ on the Cross and His resurrection.

DR. GAVERLUK: We have a lot to do. We have to get ourselves ready just like a bride does. We have to get ourselves ready spiritually, make sure we are walking with the Lord. Then we have to witness to our loved ones and make sure they have committed themselves to the Lord Jesus Christ. We have to try to win our friends to Jesus. We have a big job ahead of us, and we don't know how much time is left. Now is the time; this is the day of salvation.

Chapter Three

THE BLESSED HOPE

DR. GAVERLUK: Dr. Lindsted, can you define what the purpose of the Tribulation is, and what it is? From the Scriptures, we know that it is seven years long.

DR. LINDSTED: Right. The Word of God is clear. The Tribulation is a seven-year period of time. The aspect of the Tribulation is God's wrath pouring out upon the Earth. When Israel rejected Christ, they were cut off. Luke 13 speaks of a fig tree that bore no fruit and; therefore, was cut off. The Tribulation answers the question that men have continually asked: If there is a God, why does He continue to allow people to live the way they do? If there is a God, why does He allow war? If there is a God, why does He allow crime? In the Tribulation, God is going to judge the Earth for these things. He is simply giving a period of time, a grace period, that men might come to accept Christ. He will take home all those who have received Him and then He will pour out His wrath upon the Earth. This Tribulation will also be used to bring Israel to repentance, to bring Israel to complete recognition of Christ and the Messiah.

DR. GAVERLUK: Somebody is going to ask us where we get the idea of the seven years. We find that in Daniel 9:24: *"Seventy weeks are determined upon thy people and upon thy holy city . . . . "* Seventy weeks, that is 490 years! A week is considered to be seven years. *. . . upon thy people* (that is Israel) *and upon thy holy city* (that is Jerusalem) *. . . . "* Seventy weeks, or 490 years, will bring the climax and the introduction of the Millennium in which Israel will have a leading role. This means that seventy weeks are determined, or preprogrammed, upon your people and your holy city to: *"finish the transgression, and to make an end of sins, and to make reconciliation for iniquity, and to bring in everlasting righteousness, and to seal up the vision and prophecy, and to anoint the most Holy."* Israel is looking forward to this and so are we. It is an astounding prophecy that is given to us. By the way, that week is going to be determined by a peace treaty that will be made.

DR. LINDSTED: Yes, as you have just read in Dan. 9:27, what begins that week is a peace treaty between the Antichrist and Israel. Israel will actually trust the Antichrist to the extent that they will sign a peace treaty, they will become "unwalled."

DR. GAVERLUK: That peace treaty will actually be broken by the Antichrist, won't it?

DR. LINDSTED: Yes, I believe it will and he will bring against them a terrible time. I also believe this is the terrible time described in Revelation 12.

DR. GAVERLUK: This peace treaty is an abhorrence to God. It is not trusting God, it is trusting the Devil. That is what it really amounts to.

DR. LINDSTED: Since Christ is the Prince of Peace, the Antichrist will want to be prince of peace. He will, however, be a false prince of peace.

DR. GAVERLUK: When we look at Isaiah 28 we read that this peace treaty has already been cancelled by God. *"And your covenant with death shall be disannulled,* (Isaiah 28:18) *and your agreement with hell shall not stand; when the overflowing scourge* (of Armageddon) *shall pass through, then ye shall be trodden down by it."* It is that God already passes judgment on that particular peace treaty. What does the Tribulation then consist of? The whole book of Revelation reveals the judgments of God that fall upon planet Earth during that seven-year period.

DR. LINDSTED: Revelation 6 through 19 deals with this Tribulation, this time of refinement for Israel and the time of persecution, death and destruction on the Earth. But again, the most important thing to emphasize about the Church is that we do not go through the Tribulation.

DR. GAVERLUK: Do you see that in Revelation?

DR. LINDSTED: God very carefully shows that the Church is called out PRIOR to the Tribulation.

DR. GAVERLUK: The Church is not mentioned from chapter four until chapter nineteen.

DR. LINDSTED: That is right. He calls them out in chapter four, and the Church is not mentioned again on Earth until chapter nineteen when He comes back with them. This is an important thing for all to see. Some of the confusion that has come about as a result of this question, "Does the Church go through the Tribulation?" is often categorized by looking at what we call pre-Tribulation, mid-Tribulation and post-Tribulation. Now it is important for us to define each of these: Pre-Tribulation means prior to, or before the Tribulation. I believe in the pre-Tribulational return of Christ.

DR. GAVERLUK: That means that the Church will disappear before the seven-year period.

DR. LINDSTED: Right. Before that Tribulation period can begin, before Daniel 9:27 can be fulfilled, I believe the Church will be called out by God. We will go to meet him in the Air. Now there are some who subscribe to what is called a mid-Tribulation belief. In other words, they believe the Church will go through part of this time of testing, part of this Jacob's trouble.

DR. GAVERLUK: Doesn't that encroach on the program that God has for Israel?

DR. LINDSTED: I think it does, and I think what we can do in using chapter and verse is show how that the hope of the Christian is for the covenant Christ. The hope of the Christian is not for tribulation. We are to comfort one another with the coming of Christ, but we are not to discourage one another by saying that we have to go through even part of this Tribulation.

DR. GAVERLUK: Some people believe that the mid-Tribulation point is where the Church is actually going to be raptured?

DR. LINDSTED: Yes, some do believe that. Then there are some who even subscribe to what is called a post-Tribulational belief (the post means after the Tribulation). In other words, they believe the Church will actually go through this seven year period of Tribulation and then He will take the Church home to heaven.

And so you can see that this is an important question for several reasons. First of all, it determines what the Church will be doing for at least seven years. If the church were to stay on earth through the whole Tribulation, we would have to prepare ourselves vastly different than if we were looking for the imminent return of Christ. How we live today as Christians is directly affected by whether or not we believe Christ is coming imminently, or whether Christ is coming after the seven-year Tribulation period. How we raise our children is affected, how we work our jobs and how we face each day. All this is vastly affected by our precept of whether it is a pre-Tribulation return of Christ, a mid-Tribulation return of Christ, or a post-Tribulation return of Christ. There are literally hundreds of theories, however, we can not deal with all of them. What I want to do is take the Bible — the Old Testament pictures and words as well as the New Testament Epistles and the book of Revelation — and show how, as you bring together the scenario of God's plan, it is clearly this: the Church is removed prior to the Tribulation, before one single day, before one single second of the Tribulation, the Church is gone. Whereas God will directly deal with Israel in the Tribulation to refine them so they will be ready when Christ comes back after the Tribulation.

It would be worthwhile for us to look at the urgency with which the writers of the New Testament wrote each epistle. For example, I think we already mentioned how John wrote for the people to be ready for this. I John 3:2 says: *"Beloved, now are we the sons of God, and it doth not yet appear what we shall be: but we know that, when he shall appear, we shall be like him; for we shall see him as he is."* This aspect of the coming of Christ was what motivated John to write how they should refine their lives, how they should be pure. *". . . every man that hath this hope in him purifieth himself, even as he is pure"* (vs. 3). So he was encouraging the people to look for the soon and sudden return of Christ.

You read in James 5:8: *"Be ye also patient; stablish your hearts: for the coming of the Lord draweth nigh."* Now James is a very practical book. It talks about how a person who is really saved, really a Christian, needs to live in the light of the faith that he has professed. After going through a whole book of practical Christian living, James could say: *". . . for the coming of the Lord draweth nigh."* He doesn't say "tribulation is drawing nigh," but he says *"the coming of the Lord draweth near."* So the hope of James and John was the soon return of Christ.

Let's take a testimony of Peter in I Peter 4:7 where it says: *"But the end of all things is at hand: be ye therefore sober, and watch unto prayer."* Peter's encouragements and motivation for the people was that the fulfillment of all things is at hand. In other words, the coming of Christ is imminent.

I then think of the Apostle Paul. This is a tremendous statement he makes in Titus 2:13: *"Looking for that blessed hope, and the glorious appearing of the great God and our Savior Jesus Christ . . . ."* So Paul along with Peter, James and John, are all looking for the imminent return of Christ. It is interesting that in the last book of the Bible, the last chapter we read that three times Christ says: *". . . behold, I come quickly . . . ."* (vs. 7). In verse 12 He says: *"And, behold, I come quickly; and my reward is with me . . . ."* Then again in chapter 22, verse 20 He says: *. . . Surely I come quickly . . . ."* So we have each writer of the New Testament epistles giving testimony to the fact that there is an imminent return of Christ; therefore we are to make our lives holy.

DR. GAVERLUK: Let's look at I Peter 4:17: *"For the time is come that judgment must begin at the house of God: and if it first begin at us, what shall the end be of them that obey not the gospel of God?"* So the judgment, in a sense the Tribulation, cannot begin until it begins with us first. And how is it to begin with us? We are to be instantly caught up to meet Christ, to meet Him at our judgment. We have to be removed. I think this is a wonderful verse.

DR. LINDSTED: Yes, it really puts things into perspective as to the judgment.

DR. GAVERLUK: Peter leads up to that verse with what you were just saying, that the *"end of all things is at hand: be ye therefore sober, and watch unto prayer"* (I Peter 4:7). Here is the attitude that we must develop if we are looking forward to the Lord coming for us. We are caught up, to meet Him in the air. While we are waiting, what are we to do? Peter gives a marvelous admonition in verses 8—11: *". . . above all things have fervent love among yourselves: for love shall cover the multitude of sins. Use hospitality one to another without grudging. As every man hath received the gift, even so minister the same one to another, as good stewards of the manifold grace of God. If any man speak, let him speak as the oracles of God; if any man minister, let him do it as of the ability which God giveth: that God in all things may be glorified through Jesus Christ, to whom be praise and dominion for ever and ever . . . ."* Here is what we are talking about. We have to sharpen our lives while we have the time, right now, in preparation for that wonderful moment when we are suddenly snatched up.

DR. LINDSTED: That is right. You see the judgment for the Church is now, and it will climax and culminate at the Judgment Seat of Christ. After that point we will judge with Christ. What a striking contrast. God will continue to judge the nations and Israel during this seven-year period of Tribulation.

DR. GAVERLUK: Let's sharpen that up. If we don't take the sin out of our lives right now — we are saved but there is still sin in us, we have bad habits and are doing things we should not do — when we stand before the Lord God, (and our God is a consuming fire) it is God's holiness that is going to burn that sin. The sin is going to be taken out of us and judged. It will hurt simply because we were careless and should have done it while we had the chance under the age of grace, when we could have applied the wonderful work of salvation to our hearts. *"Work out your salvation . . . "* (Phil. 2:12) is a part of the thing we should be doing until that wonderful moment when the Lord takes us up.

DR. LINDSTED: Right, and *". . . everyone who has this hope in him purifieth himself . . . "* (I John 3:3). You see it is this hope that purifies us. As a matter of fact, it would be interesting to discuss this hope because this is an important phrase. If a person traces this through Scriptures, he will see a very unique design for the Church as opposed to Israel.

For example, we read in Ephesians 4:4: *"There is one body, and one Spirit, even as ye are called in one hope of your calling . . . ."* Now that is interesting because Paul also says in Ephesians 1:18: *"The eyes of your understanding being enlightened; that ye may know what is the hope of his calling . . . "* Here the Apostle Paul says, you've got just one hope and, furthermore, you should know what your hope is. It is interesting to talk to people and ask them what is their hope. There are some who say, "Well our hope is salvation, our hope is everlasting life." Really that is not the hope of the Christian. The reason I say that is because the hope is future. John 5:24 says: *" . . . he that believeth on him . . . hath everlasting life . . . . "* We have salvation right now, so our salvation is not really our hope. John 5:24 says: *" . . . is passed from death unto life . . . . "* We have already passed from death unto life, so salvation is a present possession, not our hope. I have even had one person tell me one time that death is our hope. I said, "no, it can't be." Here is why. In I Corinthians 15:51 it says: *" . . . We shall not all die, but we shall all be changed . . . . . "* So our hope is not salvation since that is a present possession. Our hope is not death, because we are not all going to die. But Peter in I Peter 1:3 says this: *"Blessed be the God and Father of our Lord Jesus Christ, which according to his abundant mercy hath begotten us again unto a lively hope by the resurrection of Jesus Christ from the dead."* We have a living hope. We also find that this living hope is reserved in heaven. We know according to II Thessalonians 2:16, that our hope is given to us by grace. Now what is this one hope? I believe this is where we find real meaning to the phrase that Paul gave us when he says: *"Looking for that blessed hope, and the glorious appearing of the great God and our Saviour Jesus Christ"* (Titus 2:13). We find that The church has one hope, and that hope is the appearing of Christ.

I Timothy 1:1 says: *" . . . and Lord Jesus Christ, which is our hope."* We have only one hope. Paul says, know what it is. It is reserved in heaven. And then finally he reveals it, the Blessed Hope is even the glorious appearing of the Lord Jesus Christ. That is our hope! That is what purifies us; that is what keeps us going. That is what allows us to pray that maybe even today will be the imminent return of Christ. Only the Church can say that. Israel can't say that, just the Church.

DR. GAVERLUK: Isn't that a marvelous analogy about a bride who puts on clean clothes. She washes her clothes, puts on new clothes, and then she dresses herself up beautifully so that the bridegroom will see her in her radiant best. This is exactly what you are talking about that we should be doing right now. Do not think you can do this by yourself. All you do is allow the Lord to do it. We have in Philippians 1:6: *"Being confident of this very thing, that he which hath begun a good work in you will perform it until the day of Jesus Christ . . . . "* So the Holy Spirit of God is in my body. He is already working to cleanse me and prepare me for that wonderful meeting that I will have with my Lord and Savior, Jesus Christ. What goes for me goes for everyone else, right?

DR. LINDSTED: You see how important this is. If Satan can get us thinking that we have a period of time — the Tribulation — to prepare ourselves to meet Christ, then he has done what he wants to do to every person. He has gotten them to look away from their Blessed Hope. He has also gotten them to think, I don't have to have an urgency about my life because when the

Tribulation comes, then I can really begin to be a testimony, begin to be a witness for Christ." So I believe that Satan is trying to undermine the Word of God by allowing people to believe that they have time to spend — on unspiritual things. Whereas in the Word of God, every writer of the New Testament speaks of the single hope of the believer — Christ is coming, Christ is coming soon — therefore, get your life ready just as a bride gets ready for her wedding day. I don't know of a single bride that says, "I've got a long time to get ready for my wedding." Instead she knows that during the engagement period every day counts in preparing for the wedding, so she is making progress for that every day. She is looking for that every day, and in a similar way we, as the Church, need to be looking for the return of Christ, not for the Tribulation. The Tribulation is for the world, it is for Israel, but it is NOT for the Church. Our hope is Christ.

DR. GAVERLUK: We have to start cleaning ourselves. That means getting rid of our bad habits, getting rid of the things that are hindering our spiritual development. We must be sanctified in Jesus Christ, and the Lord is giving us time. Examine your life carefully. Judge yourself now because you are going to have to face the Lord. If you don't do it now, He will do it then and it will hurt.

Chapter Four

Pre — Mid — Post — ?

DR. GAVERLUK: The paramount importance of this series is giving Scripture which supports the rapture of the Church, prior to the Tribulation. The Church will not go through the Tribulation; the Church will not even be on earth when that time comes.

DR. LINDSTED: Even though there are many theories that are being generated about pre-Tribulation, mid-Tribulation and post-Tribulation, we have to go back to the Word of God. We have to examine passages of Scripture to reach the conclusion that the Church is taken out prior to the Tribulation period, and I want us to look at several of those. The first one is in I Thessalonians 4:13-18. I know that this is a familiar portion of Scripture and it is used sometimes by those people who believe in pre-Tribulation as well as mid-Tribulation and post-Tribulation, but as we begin to examine the wording and the context of the very message that the Apostle Paul gave, I think we can see how important and how clearly it distinguishes a pre-Tribulation return of Christ for the Church. Let's read these verses: *"But I would not have you to be ignorant, brethren, concerning them which are asleep, that ye sorrow not, even as others which have no hope."* There's the hope again. Now remember we found earlier that we have one hope and that hope is the blessed return of Christ. *"For if we believe that Jesus died and rose again, even so them also which sleep in Jesus will God bring with him. For this we say unto you by the word of the Lord, that we which are alive and remain unto the coming of the Lord shall not prevent them which are asleep."* Now notice here that this is the word of the Lord, it is not just the idea of the apostle Paul. Notice it says, *" . . . we who are alive . . . "* In other words, Paul was planning to be alive when Christ came back. He was looking for the imminent return of Christ, wasn't he? Because he includes himself in that group, *"we who are alive and remain."* *"For the Lord himself shall descend from heaven with a shout, with the voice of the archangel, and with the trump of God: and the dead in Christ shall rise first: Then we which are alive and remain shall be caught up together with them in the clouds, to meet the Lord in the air: and so shall we ever be with the Lord. Wherefore comfort one another with these words."* The context under which the Apostle Paul wrote this passage is an important one. The Apostle Paul was only in Thessalonica for a short period of time, some say maybe four or five weeks, it was during this time that he covered a variety of topics, one of those was the fact that Christ was going to come back for the Church. I believe that his preaching and teaching to them was so exciting concerning the coming of Christ, that they were looking for Him to come right away. And as the weeks wore on and Christ did not come back, they began to be concerned because some in their midst had fallen asleep, or had died. So they were saying, does this mean they have missed the coming of Christ? Does this mean they have missed the hope that they have? Paul writes back and says, no, we are not like those who have no hope: we have a hope. As a matter of fact those who have died first, when Christ comes back, when He gives a shout, when they hear the voice of the archangel and the trump of God, the dead in Christ will rise first. In other words, they still have this one hope. You cannot take away this hope even with someone who has died in the church age. Then verse 17 says: *"Then we which are alive and remain shall be caught up together with them in the clouds, to meet the Lord in the air . . ."* "With them," that is Christ and those that were dead and have risen first. It is interesting that there is really no warning up until this time. He does not say you can look for a sign, because you can not. The coming of Christ is His imminent return. There is no sign that points to the coming of Christ. The signs really are for Israel, for the Tribulation period, but this is to be a surprise, or a sudden snatching away of the church.

DR. GAVERLUK: He doesn't really come to the earth, He comes to the air, and we rise up to meet him. So as you say, there is no indication at all as to how close we are to that event, by any world sign or any prophecy. There is no prophecy in regard to that.

DR. LINDSTED: Now another interesting thing about this passage, and you will find this is true of every rapture passage, there is no judgment on the earth mentioned. So I think that we draw from this several important things. First, that Paul was looking for the imminent return of Christ. He puts himself with those looking for the return of Christ, *"we who are alive and remain."* Next, this occurs in the clouds, not on the earth, which is in striking contrast to the end of the Tribulation. So I would say that as we look at this passage of Scripture, it is talking about when He will deal with the Church, and at this point in time it appears that He has no warning, but it is a sudden return.

As we begin chapter five of I Thessalonians, I want us to notice that there is a contrast here, because he says: *"But of the times and the seasons, brethren, ye have no need that I write unto you. For yourselves know* perfectly that the day of the Lord so cometh as a thief in the night." Now the day of the Lord is mentioned a variety of times in both the Old Testament and the New Testament. For example in Amos 5:16-20, Obadiah 1:15-17 and Isaiah 13:9-16, which follows: *"But the day of the Lord cometh, cruel both with wrath and fierce anger, to lay the land desolate: and he shall destroy the sinners out of it."* So when the day of the Lord comes there is judgment, but in the rapture he doesn't speak of judgment on the earth. Now as we read through I Thessalonians 4:13-18, he says, all right, here is a comfort, here is hope for those that are Christian. Then chapter five begins with the word, "But . . . " and there is a contrast. He says, you know perfectly, in other words he says, you know the plan of God as it is working out, that the day of the Lord . . . Now this is a wrath portion of Scripture. And he goes on and says, *"And when they shall say Peace and Safety . . . "* Now who is going to say that? In the Tribulation period, Israel will be under the false guide of a peace treaty that the Antichrist will make; we read that in Daniel 9:27. So when they think peace and safety has finally come, suddenly destruction will be upon them. Notice I Thessalonians 5:4: *"But ye, brethren, are not in darkness . . . "* You see the Tribulation is referred to as darkness; it is referred to as judgment, but we Christians are not in the darkness. Paul tells the Christian in verse eight: *"But let us, who are of the day, be sober, putting on the breastplate of faith and love; and for an helmet, the hope of salvation."* He is contrasting the fact that judgment comes to the world after the church is delivered or raptured. That is the nighttime, the darkness. We as Christians are children of the day. Notice in verse nine: *"For God hath not appointed us to wrath, but to obtain salvation by our Lord Jesus Christ."* In other words he said, the Christian is delivered out of wrath, but the world goes through this wrath.

DR. GAVERLUK: We want the readers to know that this verse, I Thessalonians 5:9, is a very critical verse. The *"wrath"* mentioned in this verse is the judgment of God as it is revealed in the book of Revelation and will come upon the world. However, the Lord has a way of delivering us Christians out of the world, just as He has a way of delivering Israel.

DR. LINDSTED: We are going to look at verses that actually reveal the fact that our salvation is a salvation which is free from this wrath. We never have to undergo the wrath of God as a Christian. So I believe part of the problem has been that people have not taken the context of this important book of I Thessalonians, and seen that chapters four and five really fit together. Paul first describes the rapture in chapter four; this is our last comfort, our one hope. It is a sudden appearing. It is in the clouds. Then chapter five gives the contrast; it is wrath and judgment. He tells us clearly in verses four and eight that we are children of the day. As children of the day we do not go through this judgment or this nighttime period. So I believe these are good verses to prove that the church does not go through the Tribulation period.

It is also important for us to look at another portion of Scripture which fits in well with this. It is I Corinthians 15:51 and it reads as follows: *"Behold, I shew you a mystery; We shall not all sleep, but we shall all be changed."* The mystery mentioned here is not resurrection. All of chapter 15 is dealing with the importance of resurrection, but resurrection is not a mystery. The people Paul addressed this letter to were familiar with resurrections. They saw them in the Old Testament. They saw them throughout the Gospels. They had seen them when Christ was here on the Earth. Therefore, I don't think this mystery is speaking of resurrection but rather of rapture, or the snatching out of the church. In the next verse of this chapter, verse 52, we read: *"In a moment, in the twinkling of an eye, at the last trump: for the trumpet shall sound, and the dead shall be raised incorruptible, and we shall be changed."* I believe this is speaking of the victory we have in Christ, the snatching away, or the rapture. Notice again there is really no warning. The trump shall sound suddenly and we shall be changed; we are given a new body.

Several years ago General Electric wanted to look at the twinkling of an eye. The twinkling of an eye is not the blinking of an eye, it is different. The twinkling of an eye, General Electric claims, is how long it takes for light to pass from the surface of the eye to the retina. Light travels at the rate of 186,000 miles a second. Taking that speed, a beam of light could travel from the earth to the moon and back in three seconds. That is how fast light travels. Light traveling through the retina of the eye, going from the surface of the eye to the retina of the eye, would only allow light to go 18 inches off the earth. That is how fast this twinkling of an eye is. Light that would go from the earth to the moon and back in three seconds, would only be 18 inches off the ground, and just like that we are changed. It is a sudden appearance which is not seen by the world because we meet Him in the clouds.

In both I Thessalonians and this I Corinthians passage we read of a trump. In I Corinthians 15:52 it says the last trump. Often people wonder if this is the last trump mentioned in Revelation concerning the twenty-one judgments that are poured out.

DR. GAVERLUK: THE CHOSEN PEOPLE QUESTION BOX II by Dr. Henry J. Heydt gives a good answer to this question. I will give an excerpt from this: *"When Paul wrote the letter to the Corinthian church the book of Revelation had not yet been written, and the expression would have made no sense to them if it referred to something altogether unknown. Let us credit the Scripture writers at least with the mental ability of writing intelligently to their readers. Paul is referring to a matter well known in that day — the blowing of the trumpets at the Feast of Trumpets. This took place at the synagogue at Corinth every year. Many Jews had gone there when Claudius expelled them from Rome, and Paul had witnessed to both Jews and Greeks for a year and six months (Acts 18:1-11). He had been there for the Feast of Trumpets and would certainly have explained its significance either in the synagogue or the house of Titus Justus where he taught. The feast opened with three different type blasts or trumps on the Shofar and trumpets. These were the teki'ah (long), the teru'ah (quivering) and the shebarim (short broken sounds). The Mishna says, "THE SHOFAR GAVE A LONG BLAST AND THE TRUMPETS A SHORT ONE . . . " (Rosh Hashanah 26b). A series of thirty blasts is repeated three times making ninety sounds in all. "The last tekiah was prolonged and was called 'teki'ah gedolah' — 'long teci'ah" (The Jewish Encyclopedia, article on "Shofar"). This was* the "last trump" Paul referred to in I Corinthians 15, and it has nothing to do with the seventh trumpet in Revelation. The Feast of Trumpets preceded the time of affliction portrayed by Yom Kippur (Lev. 23:24,27) and proves, by the application Paul gave to it, that the resurrection, change and catching away of believers (I Thess. 4:15-17) takes place before the time of Jacob's trouble."

DR. LINDSTED: I enjoy your sharing that article because we see that really this fits together in a very beautiful way for the sudden catching out of the church.

Another passage that is important for us to consider is in John 14:1: *"Let not your heart be troubled: ye believe in God, believe also in me."* The chapter goes on to say that Jesus has gone to prepare a place for us and He says: *". . . I will come again . . ."* This promise that He will come again is a promise that was made 50 times throughout the Gospel. He promised He would come again. It is also interesting that as He describes here, in what I believe to be a rapture passage, there is no sign given; there is a shout, the trump is sounded, and the rapture has already begun. Christ is already in the clouds so there is no time at that point for the Christians to get ready. I Corinthians 15, I Thessalonians four and five, and John 14 all point to the soon and sudden return of Christ.

In this particular chapter of this book, we are trying to show New Testament passages that point to the imminent return of Christ. In Acts 1, Jesus is speaking to His disciples about spreading the Gospel throughout the world and telling them that they will receive power to do this. Verse nine says: *"And when he had spoken these things, while they beheld, he was taken up; and a cloud received him out of their sight."* Then in verse 11 two men in white apparel, said: *". . . Ye men of Galilee, why stand ye gazing up into heaven? this same Jesus, which is taken up from you into heaven, shall so come in like manner as ye have seen him go into heaven."* The words *"like manner"* referred to in this verse are to be taken both literally and physically. Some people believe he will come back in a spiritual way. No, Christ came the first time in a physical way. He will come the second time in a physical way. It will be a literal coming back. Christ will be in the clouds as He pointed out in I Thessalonians chapter four. Notice that He was talking to those who were saved, those who trusted in Christ. Those were the ones who had the promise that He would come back and appear to them in the clouds. Not to those who were unbelieving. He did not say that to the nation of Israel. He said it to those men who had committed their lives to Him.

II Thessalonians chapter two, ties in exactly with the portions we have been looking at. It begins by saying: *"Now we beseech you, brethren, by the coming of our Lord Jesus Christ . . ."* I really think this is speaking of the rapture. Paul goes on to talk about the troubles that will come, and again he mentions the aspect of the day of the Lord. Remember we saw the day of the Lord as a time of trouble. In chapter two, verse one, we have the rapture. After the rapture, the trouble comes, the day of the Lord comes, verse two. Next there is a falling away, which I believe to be a spiritual falling away, in verse three. Verses six through eight: *"And now ye know what restraineth that he* might be revealed in his time. For the mystery of iniquity doth already work: only he who now hinders will continue to hinder, until he be taken out of the way. And then shall that Wicked One be revealed . . . "* In other words, the Wicked One cannot be revealed until the Holy Spirit is removed because the Holy Spirit is so much greater than the Wicked One. The Wicked One cannot even do his work until the Holy Spirit is taken out of the way.

DR. GAVERLUK: In closing, let's go back to I Thessalonians, chapter 4, the first 12 verses. These verses deal with the fact that our lives should be pure, holy and clean in preparation for the marvelous event of the rapture. Verse seven: *"For God hath not called us unto uncleanness, but unto holiness."* The previous verses speak of sexual abuse even in the heart of those who call themselves Christians. Verses four through six give us this warning: *"That every one of you should know how to possess his vessel in sanctification and honor; Not in the lust of concupiscence, even as the Gentiles which know not God: That no man go beyond and defraud his brother in any matter: because that the Lord in the avenger of all such, as we also have forewarned you and testified."* The implication is clear that no one is to take someone elses wife in sexual abuse, because *"the Lord is the avenger of all such . . ."*

You don't have much time to clean up your lives before the Lord comes, and while the Lord gives us time we had better confess our sins, come to the Lord in absolute repentance and cleanse ourselves so that we will be ready for that wonderful moment when suddenly we shall be caught up to meet the Lord in the air.

Chapter Five

FALSE CHRISTS

DR. LINDSTED: II Thessalonians 2 is an important passage. As we look at it, verse by verse, we see that the Holy Spirit, using the Apostle Paul, clearly points out that the Church does not go through the tribulation.

DR. GAVERLUK: The first verse says the Church is not to look for the tribulation, but for something else. *"Now we beseech you, brethren, by the coming of our Lord Jesus Christ, and by our gathering together unto him"* (II Thess. 2:1).

DR. LINDSTED: This is a beautiful description of the rapture, therefore what we have following must be what takes place after the rapture and we will begin to see how that fits the description of the Tribulation period.

For example, in verses two and three we read: *" . . . be not soon shaken in mind, or be troubled, neither by spirit, nor by word, nor by letter as from us, as that the day of Christ is at hand. Let no man deceive you by any means: for that day shall not come, except there come a falling away first, and that man of sin be revealed, the son of perdition."*

We should point out that verse three has several interpretations. There are some who see it as an additional description of the rapture and others who see it as a spiritual decline. I happen to be in the latter group, although there are many pre-Tribulation people who believe that it refers to the rapture.

DR. GAVERLUK: I believe it is a description of the rapture and I will explain why. The phrase *"the falling away first"* is from the greek word "apostasia." The question is, why didn't the Holy Spirit use the word "harpazo" as he did in I Thessalonians 4:17? The first seven English translations prior to the King James version did not translate that phrase as *"falling away."* Instead, they translated it as *"departing."* It is estimated that of those first seven translations, 70 to 80 percent of the content carried forward to the King James translation. In this portion of the King James, the *"falling away"* was used instead of *"departing."* By going back to the first verse of chapter 4, we establish the context. The first verse concerns the coming of Christ and our gathering together unto him. The word "apostasia" would have significance not just for the Church. If the word "harpazo" would have been used, it would have meant strickly for the Church. If that had been the case, remnant Israel would have felt that God had left them out. There is an utter finality to the word "harpazo." "Apostasia" has within it the components of: falling away; judgment; abomination; urgency. In II Thessalonians 2:3, the usage of this word is that of urgency. In Matthew 24:16, Mark 13:14 and Luke 27:21, it is the Messiah who says to those in Judea to "flee" when they see the man of sin; the abomination of desolation. It is again that meaning of urgency.

It is also significant for the tribulation saints to know that "apostasia" means the abomination is coming. They will have to die. But when they look at Revelation, chapter 20, they will read that they will be raised to rule and reign with Christ in the Millennium. So the word "apostasia" has a special significance to them; they are not left out.

What's more, it has a very special significance to every Christian generation who looks forward to being reunited with their loved ones. When will you be reunited with your loved ones? It will be at the time when the abomination is going to occur. In that day, the resurrection is going to occur and you will see your loved ones. It is a specific point in time — the abomination.

DR. LINDSTED: This is certainly a passage that I will have to study further because you make some interesting points that I would like to consider. I have always viewed these verses as: Chapter two, verse one — the rapture; verses two and three — the apostasy or falling away. What you have brought out is that it is really a much broader sense than that. It is interesting that with either point of view, one would still come to the pre-Tribulation return of Christ for the church.

As we come to verses five and six, Paul writes: *"Remember ye not, that, when I was yet with you, I told you these things? And now ye know what withholdeth that he might be revealed in his time."* Paul is saying that there is something at work today that prevents the Antichrist from having his way in the world. I believe that to be the Spirit of God. I John 4:4 says: *". . . greater is he that is in you, than he that is in the world."* So the Holy Spirit restrains the Antichrist and Satan from doing his great work. Verse seven tells us that he is already at work, he just cannot do it to the degree he would like to.

"For the mystery of iniquity doth already work; only he who now letteth will let, until he be taken out of the way." I think that is the spirit of God, active and working in the Church, preventing the Antichrist from coming.

Notice verse eight: *"And then shall that Wicked one be revealed, whom the Lord shall consume with the spirit of his mouth, and shall destroy with the brightness of his coming."* I think it is important for people to recognize that the Wicked One cannot come until after the Holy Spirit, or that which restrains, has been removed. That will occur at the catching out of the Church.

DR. GAVERLUK: Of course, that is the Holy Spirit in us. When He steps aside, that means he takes us. So in effect, our presence is restraining the Antichrist.

DR. LINDSTED: That is correct because the spirit of God is in us. As long as the Church is here, the Antichrist cannot do what he would like to do because *"greater is he that is in you, than he that is in the world."*

It continues in verse eight to say: *" . . . Whom the Lord shall consume with the spirit of his mouth, and shall destroy with the brightness of his coming."* That is none other than Satan and the Antichrist.

Verse 10 and 11 read: *"And with all deceivableness of unrighteousness in them that perish; because they received not the love of the truth, that they might be saved. And for this cause God shall send them strong delusion, that they should believe a lie."*

I think we have made an important point here for the pre-Tribulation return of Christ, and we need to emphasize this fact. The flow of this passage indicates that the rapture occurs, then the antichrist is revealed and his work begins in a great way. If we were left on Earth, we could even be deceived because of his great power, But because the Spirit of God is in us and because we are taken out, we are protected from the Antichrist.

DR. GAVERLUK: It is amazing that back in Matthew 24, Jesus gives three verses regarding this. *"For many shall come in my name, saying, I am Christ; and shall deceive many"* (Matt. 24:5. In verse 11 we read: *"And many false prophets shall rise, and shall deceive many."* And continuing in verse 24: *"For there shall arise false Christs, and false prophets, and shall shew great signs and wonders; insomuch that, if it were possible, they shall deceive the very elect."* In other words, one of the greatest signs of the coming of Christ is that you will see these false Christs coming, and that is certainly exploding right in our time.

DR. LINDSTED: Let us continue with Matthew 24, because that is another verse that I think has some interesting things to show us concerning the pre-Tribulation of Christ.

Verse 8 says: *"All these are the beginning of sorrows."* What is being described as *"the beginning of sorrows"* is discussed in verses 4 through 7, and they are speaking of the first of the Tribulation. But notice in verse 9: *"Then shall they deliver you up to be afflicted . . . ."* Now we begin a tremendous persecution that occurs in the middle of the Tribulation, or in the *"midst of the week"* as we saw when we were reading Daniel 9:27 regarding the breaking of the covenant. This breaking of the covenant will bring a great affliction upon Israel. It is also the time described in Revelation 12 when Satan is cast out of Heaven, restricted to Earth, and he brings great fury, wrath and persecution against Israel. Therefore, these verses line up Matthew 24:9.

Notice verse 21 of Matthew 24: *"For then shall be great tribulation . . . "* That again tells us when. He is not changing time frames. Verses 9 and 21 are pointing to the same period of time. When is that time? It is in the midst of the Tribulation.

Verse 22 reads: *"And except those days should be shortened, there should no flesh be saved; but for the elect's sake those days shall be shortened."* That begins Israel's time to flee. when they flee, that is a sign of the mid-Tribulation.

DR. GAVERLUK: That is when they flee to Petra.

DR. LINDSTED: That is right, and as we go on to verse 29 we read: *"Immediately after the tribulation of those days . . . . "* So now we are through with the Tribulation. Verse 30 says: *"And then shall appear the sign of the son of man in heaven: and then shall all the tribes of the earth mourn, and they shall see the Son of man coming in the clouds of heaven with power and great glory."*

DR. GAVERLUK: We are going to be part of that sign.

DR. LINDSTED: That is right. So if we look at this, it is a beautiful way to see the whole scenario. Verses 4-7 are the first part of the Tribulation. After we read those verses, we are told in verse 8 that they are the beginning of sorrows. In verse 9 the writer speaks of the mid-point in the Tribulation. The great persecution will fall; the Antichrist will bring about great desolation. Notice verse 15: *"When ye therefore shall see the abomination of desolation, spoken of by Daniel the prophet . . . . "* So he gives us that time frame. It is exactly the portion that we looked at earlier as we read Daniel 9:27. Daniel said there will be this abomination of desolation. so when is it? Verses 9 through 21 tell us that it will occur at the mid-point of the Tribulation.

If we jump down to verse 29, we read of the end of the tribulation: *"Immediately after the tribulation of those days . . . . "* and on in verse 30: *"And then shall appear the sign of the Son of man in heaven; and then shall all the tribes of the earth mourn, and they shall see the Son of man coming in the clouds of heaven with power and great glory."* So in Matthew 24 we have laid out for us God's plan for both the church and for Israel, but we must see clearly how He is dealing with Israel in the Tribulation. The Tribulation is NOT for the Church.

We summarize the points that we have been making: The coming for the Church is sudden, there are really no signs for it. Next, the coming for the Church is in the clouds. In contrast when He comes for Israel, He will come on the Earth.

DR. GAVERLUK: I think while looking at Matthew 24 we should also note the parable that Jesus gives in verses 44-48: *"Therefore be ye also ready: for in such an hour as ye think not the son of man cometh. Who then is a faithful and wise servant, whom his lord hath made ruler over his household, to give them meat in due season? Blessed is that servant, whom his Lord when he cometh shall find so doing."* If you look at the last two verses of this chapter you find: *"The lord of that servant shall come in a day when he looketh not for him, and in an hour that he is not aware of, And shall cut him asunder, and appoint him his portion with the hypocrites: there shall be weeping and gnashing of teeth."*

Beloved, we must cleanse ourselves and be ready for the Lord Jesus Christ. *"Believe on the Lord Jesus Christ, and thou shalt be saved."* Confess your sins to him now, while you have the time.

Chapter Six

OLD TESTAMENT MODELS

DR. GAVERLUK: We have been looking in the New Testament at passages concerning the rapture of the Church. Now let's turn to the Old Testament and pick up a few scriptures there.

DR. LINDSTED: What I want to do is take several characters in the Old Testament and notice how God uses them as a model, or a picture, that we can learn from, even today. I Corinthians chapter 10 tells us that we are to learn from the Old Testament. In verse 11 we read: *"Now all these things happened unto them for ensamples: and they are written for our admonition . . . "* I like to think of the Old Testament as God's picture book. When we come to the New Testament, God explains the pictures which have been painted, or portrayed, in the Old Testament.

DR. GAVERLUK: We can not ignore the precedents that we have in the Old Testament of the rapture. In Genesis 5:24 we read of Enoch: *"And Enoch walked with God: and he was not; for God took him"* and II Kings 2:11: *"And it came to pass, as they still went on, and talked, that, behold, there appeared a chariot of fire, and horses of fire, and parted them both asunder; and Elijah went up by a whirlwind into heaven."* So there we have two men who are alive from the Old Testament days who are now up in space. We could add a third who died but was raised to appear on the Mount of Transfiguration with Elijah, and that of course, was Moses.

DR. LINDSTED: If we begin to look at the whole picture of rapture, we have Enoch and Elijah. We know as well that the apostle Paul was caught up. In Revelation, chapter four, John speaks of how he was also caught up. Christ was raptured, taken up, in Acts, chapter one. The two witnesses spoken of in the book of Revelation, chapter II, will be raptured. So the Church has many patterns to study concerning the fact that Christ has the power to take, to snatch out, the Church.

Let's use Noah as our first example of a model, or a picture, in the Old

GENESIS 5

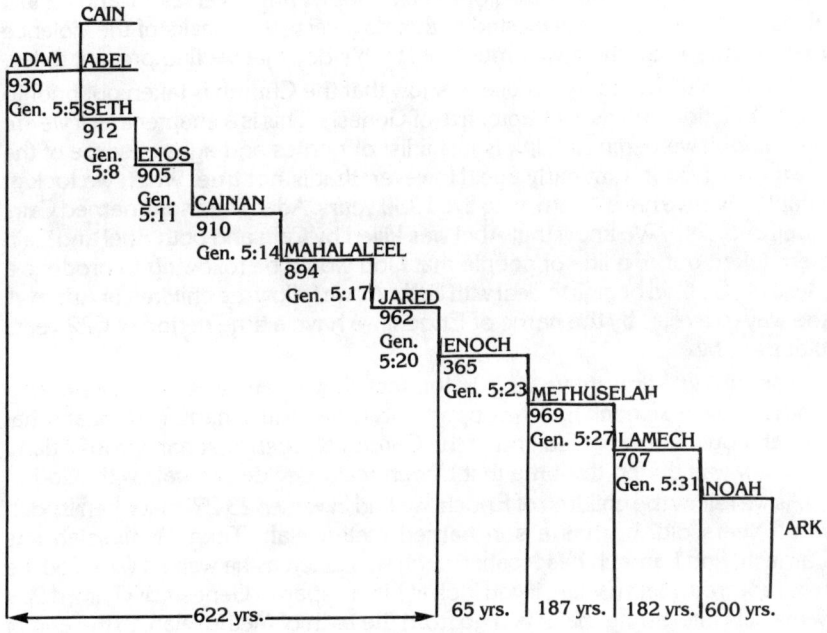

Testament. The story of Noah is in chapters five and six of Genesis. It is interesting that when we read the New Testament book of Matthew, the 24th chapter and the 37th verse, we find *"But as the days of Noah were, so shall also the coming of the Son of man be."* There are several things that existed in Noah's day, that exist as well today. One of the things we find in Genesis, chapter six, is the fact that the population was increasing at a rapid rate. Another thing we see in chapter six is mixed marriages, verse two: *"That the sons of God saw the daughters of men that they were fair; and they took them wives of all which they chose."* Verse five: *" . . . every imagination of the thoughts of his heart was only evil continually."* Verses 11 and 12 talk about the corruption that existed in that day; verse 11 speaks of the violence that was there. So there was much of Noah's day that we find present today.

The model I would like to use to show that the Church is taken out prior to the Tribulation begins in chapter five of Genesis. This is a chapter that if we are not careful, we begin to think is just a list of names and ages of some of the men who lived in that early age. However, that is not true. When we look at chapter five, we have Adam, who lived 930 years. Adam had sons named Cain, Abel, and Seth. We know that Abel was killed by Cain and both Abel and Cain were taken out of a line of people that God would be following to produce a Messiah. So God begins to deal with Seth. As we follow the children of Adam all the way to a man by the name of Enoch, we have a time period of 622 years that pass by.

Something I find interesting is the fact that Adam was still alive during Enoch's life. So Enoch had the opportunity to visit with Adam. This means that Enoch could know of God and of the Garden of Eden, first hand from Adam. Maybe it was during this time that Enoch really decided to walk with God.

As we follow the children of Enoch, we find in verses 23-27, that when Enoch is 65 years old, he has a son named Methuselah. Then Methuselah has Lamech, and Lamech has Noah. Enoch was taken as he walked with God; he was raptured. Methuselah, if you look at his life span in Genesis 5:27, lived 969 years. It is interesting that if you go from the birth of Methuselah, to the end of 969 years, he died exactly in the year of the flood. So let's take Enoch, Methuselah, and Noah and see if we can build a picture. Enoch is a picture of those people who believed God, and were raptured, or taken out. Methuselah is a picture of those people who lived right up until the time, and then died preceeding the coming of Christ. Noah is a picture of the Jewish people; he is preserved through the judgment, through this Tribulation period, by a preserving ark. It is also interesting as you continue to view this model, or picture, that the name Methuselah means *"when he dies, it shall come."* Why would Enoch name his son, *"when he dies, it shall come"* except for the fact it was God's way of showing the plan for the coming ages.

DR. GAVERLUK: Tell us how you feel the rapture is connected with these people back there in typology.

DR. LINDSTED: I would say that Noah is a picture of the nation of Israel and how God will preserve them through a terrible time. This time in Noah's day was the flood; the time in our coming day, is the time of Jacob's trouble. Enoch is a picture of the Church. He is the one who was invited to come up with God. He walked with God and he was taken, or raptured. There was no warning given for the snatching away of Enoch, just as there is no warning given for the Church. However, for Noah and for the picture of the Jewish people, there is plenty of warning. Matthew 24 tells us that the signs given in Noah's day will be the same signs existing in the final days. The signs given to Noah, parallel those of today and are a warning to the world and the Jewish people but the Church will be snatched away just as Enoch was snatched away.

Another model I like to consider in Genesis, is chapters 40 and 41. This is the character of Joseph. Of all the characters portrayed throughout the bible, and the Old Testament especially, I feel the character of Joseph portrays the life of Christ better than any other. Some say that there are over 100 parallels between the life of Joseph and the life of Christ. For example, Joseph was sold by his own brothers, just as Christ was sold by one of his own deciples, and by his Jewish brethren, and Christ has been rejected by the Jewish people. There are many parallels between the life of Christ and the life of Joseph, these are but a few, and they clearly show that Joseph is a picture of Christ. One of the things that happened to Joseph that is very interesting is the fact that when he was in his thirties, he received a wife. In Genesis 41:45-46 we read that Joseph is given a gentile bride. So between the rejection of his brothers and before he reveals himself to them he receives his gentile bride.

We see that Christ really goes beyond the typology because Joseph did not have to give his life for his brothers, but Christ loved the Church so much, loved His gentile bride so much, that He willingly gave His life.

We see that Noah, Methuselah and Enoch are one picture, or one model, in the Old Testament of how some will be raptured prior to the flood, or Tribulation. Joseph is another picture, this one showing that Christ would choose a gentile bride between the time of his rejection by his brothers and his revealing himself to his brothers.

Another character in the Old Testament is the character of Moses. In Exodus, chapters two through four, between the time of the rejection of Moses by his people, and the time of Moses leading them out of bondage in Egypt, he is given a bride. This is a gentile bride. This again, is a clear picture of how Christ will take a gentile bride before he goes back to deliver the nation of Israel.

When we go to the book of Ruth we find another model that I would like to look at. The book of Ruth is an excellent Prophetic type of New Testament Christianity because Ruth is a gentile bride. She is going to marry a Jew, or really, a redeemer kinsman. The story of Ruth occurs during the years of the judges. It is between the time Israel is governed by judges and the time they will have a king rule over them. In a parallel way, it is a picture between the period of the law, that we know was fulfilled by Christ, and when Christ comes back to reign as king. During that period of time, Christ will choose a gentile bride.

As we continue to look at the book of Ruth, we find Naomi. I believe Naomi pictures the children of Israel. She chooses to go and live among the gentile nations, just as Israel was scattered. Naomi decided it would be better to live in Moab than it would be to dwell in "the house of bread." Bethlehem — Judah literally means, "the house of bread." So Elimelech, her husband, and Naomi, loose their land. They loose the promises that God had given them. While they are out of the land, the story of the gentile bride, the story of Ruth, comes into being.

It is also interesting that a famine fell over the land. Prophetically, the nation of Israel has had a real famine. For 1,878 years there was not a nation of Israel. They are still having a spiritual famine. They have not found their Messiah because their Messiah was none other than Christ.

When Naomi comes back from the land of Moab, she asks not to be called Naomi, which means pleasant, but instead to be called Mara, which means bitter. As she comes back, notice that there are two hopeful daughters-in-law. One is Orpah. Perhaps she represents those who rejected the picture of Christ as portrayed in the Old Testament, the Islam people. It is through Christianity that they draw much of their belief but they still reject the Messiah. The other daughter-in-law is Ruth, who is a picture of true Christianity. It is interesting that Naomi's son who married Ruth is named Mahlon, which means sick or weak. So it is while Israel is sick or weak that the gentile bride comes into existance.

All of this is interesting but I think the real point to be made is this: Ruth is willing to accept the promises of God. She says to Naomi in verse 16 of chapter one: *"Entreat me not to leave thee, or to return from following after thee: for whither thou goest, I will go; and where thou lodgest, I will lodge: thy people shall be my people, and thy God my God."* In other words, Christianity came to a place where they were willing to accept what God said. Christians were willing to accept His word as the inspired word of God. In chapter two Ruth begins to work in the harvest field of the world because the harvest is ready to prepare. In verse 16 we read: *"And let fall also some of the handfuls of purpose for her, and leave them, that she may glean them, and rebuke her not."* I believe this is a picture of the age of grace. All of this comes to a climax as Boaz, the owner of the plantation, finally decides to claim Ruth as his bride. So Boaz, a redeemer kinsman, now comes and takes and marries Ruth. She becomes a joint heir of the very field where once she was a gleaner. In order to be a redeemer kinsman, you had to be free. You could not be under bondage. You would have to be willing and you would have to be wealthy. Christ really qualified in all of these ways.

We have looked at Noah, Enoch and Methuselah to see a beautiful picture of how the Church will be snatched up just as Enoch was before the great Tribulation. We looked at Moses and Joseph and the fact that they both received a gentile bride before they were allowed to be revealed to their brothers as their redeemer. We looked at Ruth, a gentile bride, and how she fits into the plan of God, how she has a redeemer kinsman. These are some models we find in the Old Testament that picture this important event of the rapture.

It is only when we get a clear picture of how the Church is taken out prior to the Tribulation that we have the urgency of living the proper lifestyle. We need to live lives that are pleasing unto God. As the bride of Christ we need to be excited about His return. We need to be readying ourselves that when he does appear,

He will be able to say "well done thou good and faithful servant" and that He will be pleased with us, as his bride, at his appearing.

DR. GAVERLUK: The patterns we see in the Old Testament, the examples, have been set for us by these people who have lived in the days gone by. They lived without the New Testament revelation we have today and yet, as Abraham, they looked forward to a city that was not made by man but by God. It is exciting that we are going to meet these people who have been examples for us in this, our New Testament day. How about you? Are you going to be an example for someone?

Chapter Seven

THE SEVEN FEASTS OF ISRAEL

DR. GAVERLUK: In this chapter we are going to look at the Feasts of Israel. They reflect the timetable of scheduled events as the Bible projects them.

DR. LINDSTED: The Feasts, like the characters we read of in the previous chapter, show a beautiful picture of the Church being taken away prior to the Tribulation period.

As we turn to the Old Testament, we find that seven feasts are recorded for Israel. These portray the way God not only works with Israel, but also the way He works with His bride, the Church. For example, in the first feast, the Passover Feast, as described in Exodus 12:1-14, a male lamb was chosen. It was kept for 14 days to ensure that it was without blemish. At the end of those 14 days, it was slain. The blood of the lamb was then put on the two side posts and on the upper door posts of the houses of the Israelites. If we take a New Testament parallel to that, we see that the Old Testament Feast of the Passover, is a picture of Calvary. For example, I Corinthians 5:7: *"Purge out therefore the old leaven, that ye may be a new lump, as ye are unleavened. For even Christ our passover is sacrificed for us."* So the New Testament shows that the sacrifice that was made for our sins by Christ, on Calvary, is really a fulfillment of the Passover.

DR. GAVERLUK: The Old Testament Passover Feast represented the fact that the blood of the sacrificial lamb was put on the doorposts, to represent that this was a Hebrew family and that the first born was covered by the blood of the lamb, therefore, he would not die. This is a wonderful typology of the New Testament at Calvary, where the blood of Jesus was shed to cover our sins.

DR. LINDSTED: We look next at the Feast of Unleavened Bread. It is described in the Old Testament in Exodus 12:15-18: *"Seven days shall ye eat unleavened bread; even the first day ye shall put away leaven out of your houses: for whosoever eateth leavened bread from the first day until the seventh day that soul shall be cut off from Israel. And in the first day there shall be a holy convocation, and in the seventh day there shall be a holy convocation to you; no manner of work shall be done in them, save that which every man must eat, that only may be done in them, save that which*

THE OLD TESTAMENT FEASTS

1. Passover (Exod. 12:14)
   Calvary (I Cor. 5:7)
2. Unleavened Bread (Exod. 12:15-18)
   Remembrance Table (I Cor. 5:8)
3. Firstfruits (Exod. 23:19)
   Resurrection (I Cor. 15:20)
4. Pentecost (Lev. 23:15-21)
   Church Formed (Acts 2:1)

INTERVAL

5. Trumpets (Lev. 23:23-25)
   Rapture (I Cor. 15:52)
6. Atonement (Lev. 16:30)
   Glorious Appearing (Heb. 9:28)
7. Tabernacles (Exod. 23:16)
   Millennium (Rev. 20:1-6)

every man must eat, that only may be done of you. And ye shall observe the feast of unleavened bread; for in this selfsame day have I brought your armies out of the land of Egypt: therefore shall ye observe this day in your generations by an ordinance for ever. In the first month, on the fourteenth day of the month at even, ye shall eat unleavened bread, until the one and twentieth day of the month at even."

The New Testament counterpart for this is found in I Corinthians 5:8 and also I Corinthians, chapter 11. I Corinthians 5:8 is as follows: *"Therefore let us keep the feast, not with old leaven, neither with the leaven of malice and wickedness; but with the unleavened bread of sincerity and truth."* We remember that before Christ left his disciples, he instituted what we call the Last Supper. So the remembrance table is pictured in the Feast of the Unleavened Bread.

The Passover is a picture of Calvary; the Unleavened Bread is a picture of our remembrance for Christ. The next feast we are going to look at is in Exodus 23:19. This talks about the Feast of the First Fruits. In I Corinthians 15:20 we read: *"But now is Christ risen from the dead, and become the first fruits of them that slept."* I believe the First Fruit Feast pictures the resurrection of Christ.

In Leviticus, chapter 23, the fourth feast is introduced. This is the Feast of Pentecost, and again we find a New Testament counterpart in Acts, chapter two, when the Church is formed.

These first four feasts, the Feast of Passover, the Unleavened Bread Feast, the First Fruit Feast, and the Feast of Pentecost, represent the time from Christ's death at Calvary to the forming of the Church. On the Jewish calendar, these first four feasts occupy only the first three months of the year. Between the fourth feast and the fifth feast, however, we have the longest interval of the calendar year. Though the first four feasts only took three months, there would be a four month interval before the fifth feast, the Feast of Trumpets. I believe this fifth feast is a picture of the rapture.

All of the feasts were prophetic. They all pointed to the coming of Christ, and his second coming. What is so beautiful about these feasts is not only do they depict Christ at Calvary, His suffering, His resurrection, the Church form, but he also tells us that the Church age is the longest period of time. Then with a blast of the trumpet, the Feast of Trumpets, the Church will be taken out.

The sixth feast is the Feast of Atonement. This corresponds to the glorious appearing of Christ which occurs after the Tribulation.

The seventh feast, the Feast of Tabernacle, is a picture of the millennial reign when Christ will come as king. The Jewish people will have been brought back to Christ; they will see Him for who He really is. Then will be His glorious reign.

These feasts which the Jewish people have celebrated for years, are a picture of what Christ is doing even in this day and time. One of the thrills for the Jewish people will come after the Church is gone. The Jewish people will realize that all of these typologies they have been reading and studying for years, point to Jesus Christ and the fact that He is the true Messiah.

DR. GAVERLUK: In Zechariah 12:10 we have a rather amazing prophecy: *"I will pour upon the house of David, and upon the inhabitants of Jerusalem, the spirit of grace and supplications: and they shall look upon me whom they have pierced, and they shall mourn for him, as one mourneth for his only son, and shall be in bitterness for him, as one that is in bitterness for his first born."* What is astonishing about this is that between the word *"me"* and the word *"whom" " . . . they shall look upon me whom . . . "* there are two letters from the Hebrew. It is not translated into the English, but it is there in the Hebrew. It is the first letter of the alphabet and the last letter of the alphabet; the *"Aleph"* and the *"Tau."* That reflects its New Testament counterpart in the book of Revelation when Christ tells us that He is the *"Alpha and Omega"* which, of course, are the first and last letters of the Greek alphabet. There is going to be an amazing rebirth of Israel at the moment they see and recognize their Messiah.

DR. LINSTED: I would like to briefly mention a few other typologies. In John 2:1 we read: *"And the third day there was a marriage in Cana of Galilee . . ."* As we look at the gospel of John, we see that the first two days Christ is involved in taking disciples and getting followers. The next day, the third day, we see a marriage. For two thousand years, or those two days, Christ getting his followers; He has been getting a bride, his Church. At the beginning of the third day, Christ is going to be involved in a wedding. That will be the wedding of Christ to his gentile bride, the Church.

Another picture we find in the gospel of John is in chapter four. In verse four we read that Jesus went through Samaria. When he was there he had dealings with a woman at the well, verses six and seven. Before the day is over, the woman comes to accept Christ as Savior. When she goes back to her people, the Samaritans, she tells them of what happened and encourages them to go and see him. In verse 40: *"So when the Samaritans were come unto him, they besought him that he would tarry with them: and he abode there two days."* He stays two days and then He goes back to deal with the Jewish people again. What a beautiful picture that is. Christ takes two days, or two thousand years, to deal with the non-Jew. Then He comes back to deal with the Jewish people again.

DR. GAVERLUK: Do you think David is a typology?

DR. LINDSTED: Yes I do. As you look at David, you see that he killed a bear and a lion. I believe that is a picture of how Israel has been freed from a lion; that would be England, and freed from a bear; that would be Russia. Then he would have his greatest battle, which would be against Goliath, who represents the battle of Armageddon. It is Christ who gave David the strength to carry on in these battles and it will be Christ who will be the strength for Israel. Without God's intervention, Israel was really not physically able to handle the lion, or bear and certainly not Goliath, but God is able. David gave God credit for every victory, and there will come a day when the new David, which is the nation of Israel, will give credit to God for victory.

DR. GAVERLUK: At one time I did not pay much attention to the book of Psalms because David wrote most of the Psalms. I thought because David was a sinner, a murderer, an adulterer, that I really wanted to have nothing to do with him. One morning, however, as I was thinking about this, a thought came to me and it seemed as if God spoke to me. I began to realize David represents Israel. That is why the Lord is going to be patient with Israel, and ultimatley save Israel just as He saved David.

I happened to be listening to the radio not long after that and heard a minister say that the Antichrist was spoken of in Psalms, chapter 52. immediately opened my Bible to Psalms 52:1-5, and read: *"Why boasteth thou thyself in mischief, O mighty man? The goodness of God endureth continually. Thy tongue deviseth mischiefs; like a sharp razor, working deceitfully. Thou lovest evil more than good; and lying rather than to speak righteousness. Thou lovest all devouring words, O thou deceitful tongue God shall likewise destroy thee for ever, he shall take thee away, and pluck thee out of thy dwelling place, and root thee out of the land of the living.* After reading this I began to wonder if perhaps there was something written prior to this concerning the resurrection, the rapture, or the Tribulation. As began searching the scriptures I found in Psalms 50:3 *"Our God shall come and shall not keep silence: a fire shall devour before him, and it shall be very tempestuous round about him."* I immediately thought of Revelation chapter 19, because this is a small picture of what happens in that chapter. As we continue to verse four of Psalms, chapter 59 we read: *"He shall call to the heavens from above, and to the earth, that he may judge his people."* began to wonder if this was referring to Israel or to the Church and I got the answer in the next verse. Verse five: *"Gather my saints together unto me those that have made a covenant with me by sacrifice."* We do not sacrifice so this speaks of Israel. I went to the Hebrew version to study this more closely and to my astonishment the Hebrew says: *"He shall call to those in the heavens to come judge His people."* I was really amazed when I read this. It is telling us that the Church is now in the heavens, and will be called to come judge His people, which is Israel. This means the Church has previously been raptured because it is already in Heaven.

DR. LINDSTED: In connection with that, remember we looked earlier at Daniel 9:24-27, which tells us about the 70 weeks or the 70 sevens. It reads as follows: *"Seventy weeks are determined upon thy people and upon thy holy city . . ."*

The critical question is, does *"thy people"* refer to Israel or to the Church? It would have to be Israel, just as the pattern we just saw in Psalms. Another question is, what would the Holy City be? It wouldn't be concerning the Church, it wouldn't be Washington, D.C. or Los Angeles, but instead, I believe it is Jerusalem. We go on to read of seven things which were to happen: *" . . . to finish the transgression, and to make an end of sins, and to make reconciliation for iniquity, and to bring in everlasting righteousness, and to seal up the vision and prophecy, and to anoint the most Holy."* Those things will not come until the 70 sevens are completed. These verses say that God will deal with the Jewish people, all the way through the 70 sevens. It does not say, however, that He is going to deal with the Church through all 70 sevens.

DR. GAVERLUK: The Church is not in the picture here.

DR. LINDSTED: That is right, it is not there at all. If we go back to an important Old Testament passage in Jeremiah 30:7, we find: *"Alas! for that day is great, so that none is like it: it is even the time of Jacob's trouble; but he shall be saved out of it."*

I once had someone ask how you can be sure that when you read of Jacob's trouble, it is speaking of Israel. In Ezekiel 20:5, we read: *"And say unto them, Thus saith the Lord God; In the day when I chose Israel, and lifted up mine hand unto the seed of the house of Jacob, and made myself known unto them in the land of Egypt, when I lifted up mine hand unto them, saying, I am the Lord your God."* So we find that the Bible refers to Israel as *"the house of Jacob,"* but there is not a single time when the Church is referred to as Jacob or the house of Jacob.

Daniel 9:24-27, is talking about what will come upon Israel. What is interesting about those verses is that they say that during a period of 490 years, Christ will come; and He will be cut off. That has already happened. It goes on to say the Jewish people would be cut off and the city would be destroyed. Then the scripture says that before that 490 years is over, before the people of Israel and their Holy city are brought into their proper place, as described in verse 24, the Antichrist will have to come and confirm the covenant with many for one week. So if we take these scriptures we find God's plan for the Church and for Israel. They are seperate plans; they are distinct, and yet they run with each other throughout the pattern of scripture.

DR. GAVERLUK: At this point in time as far as Daniel, chapter nine is concerned, the Church is not in the picture. Evidently, she has to be removed before God can take up the cause of Israel and work with her.

DR. LINDSTED: That's right. He will take up the Church so He can again deal with Israel, because He must accomplish what He said He would do in Daniel 9:24.

DR. GAVERLUK: It is astonishing that we are talking about events that will occur in our time; in our period. I think we are a lucky generation. We are going to see the darkness all around us as it grows darker and darker. Then, all of a sudden, we will have the brilliance of the light, with the coming of Christ for His own.

DR. LINDSTED: It's interesting that when Christ was born the first time, God put an extra bright light in the sky. When he died, God darkened the earth. When Christ comes back, however, the celestial bodies will be darkened out, so that nothing will compete with His great glory as He comes.

DR. GAVERLUK: That is Great! It is going to be wonderful. We hope everyone reading this is ready for this wonderful event. To hear the shout from space; the sound of the trumpet; the dead to be raised first. We have a wonderful prospect.

DR. LINDSTED: We have a living hope and we hope all our readers have that hope also.

Chapter Eight

REVELATION OF JESUS CHRIST

DR. LINDSTED: In this final chapter, we are going to be looking at the Revelation of Jesus Christ. We have recorded in the book of Revelation, a beautiful picture of Christ. It is interesting that when we read the gospels, we do not find a physical description of Christ. When we come to the Revelation, however, we have the best picture of Christ, found anywhere in the New Testament. In Revelation 1:11-15, we have the best description of Christ; we see Christ in all of His glory. God saw fit not to show us what Christ looked like humanly, but He shows us what He looks like in His glory. So the Revelation of Jesus Christ is really the glory of God, the beauty of Christ.

Even though the book of Revelation has, for many years, been difficult for some to understand, there are certain things about it that make it beautiful and fun to read and understand. For example, in Chapter one, verse 19, we have a divine outline for the entire book; *"Write the things which thou has seen, and the things which are, and the things which shall be hereafter."* So we have three divisions. Division one: *". . . the things which thou has seen . . ."* In other words, the past. This is referring to chapter one of Revelation. Division two: *". . . the things which are . . ."* This is present tense, the things which are happening right now. I believe this is referring to Revelation, chapters two and three because they describe the Church age. That's what was in process when John was writing the Revelation. Division three: *". . . the things which shall be hereafter."* This is speaking of chapters four through 22. It is interesting that the scripture uses the word *"meta tauta"* which means, hereafter. As we go to chapter four, verse one we read: *"After this I looked, and behold, a door was opened in heaven: and the first voice which I heard was as it were of a trumpet talking with me; which said, Come up hither, and I will show thee things which must be hereafter."* As we have already mentioned, the voice; the trumpet; the invitation to come up; are all a picture of the rapture of the Church. John is a picture of the Church in that case.

In summary, the Spirit of God gives us this divine outline in Revelation 1:19: (1) Past things; (2) Present Age or Church Age (Rev. 2-3); (3) Things Which Are Hereafter (Rev. 4-22).

Notice the rapture of the Church comes in chapter four, prior to the Tribulation; prior to the unveiling of the Antichrist.

DR. GAVERLUK: I keep looking back at Revelation 3:10: *"Because thou hast kept the word of my patience, I also will keep thee from the hour of temptation, which shall come upon all the world, to try them that dwell upon the earth."* The word *"from"* mentioned in this passage, is the greek word *"ek"* which means *"to be kept out of."* This is the promise that was given to the Church, and with that, the fourth chapter brings to pass the actual rapture of the Church.

DR. LINDSTED: Let's further examine the usage of the word *"from."* In Romans 5:9: *"Much more then, being now justified by his blood, we shall be saved from wrath through him."* Again the greek word *"ek"* is used for the word *"from."* When we accept Christ as savior, we never have to go through the wrath of God.

We find a similar use of the word *"from"* in I Thessalonians 1:9: *" . . . ye turned to God from idols to serve the living and true God."* Some read this passage and think the word *"from"* means *"through;"* *" . . . ye turned to God through idols."* If this were the case, the greek word used would be *"en."* The word used here, however, is *"apo"* which means *"away from."* As we look at verse 10 we read: *"And to wait for his Son from heaven, whom he raised from the dead, even Jesus, which delivered us from the wrath to come."* The Bible clearly tells the Christian that he does not go through the wrath of God.

Going to Revelation, chapters 6, 14, 16 and 19, we read of the wrath of God being poured out upon the earth. Remember, the Church is promised to be saved from the wrath of God; we are saved from the hour of temptation. If we are saved from the hour of temptation; saved from wrath; and the Tribulation is the wrath of God; how in the world can the Church be on the earth during the Tribulation? What a comfort it is to know we are saved from this.

DR. GAVERLUK: When we also look at Revelation 5:8-10: *"When he had taken the book, the four beasts and four and twenty elders fell down before the Lamb, having every one of them harps, and golden vials full of odors, which are the prayers of saints. And they sung a new song, saying, Thou are worthy to take the book, and to open the seals thereof: for thou wast slain, and hast redeemed us to God by thy blood out of every kindred, and tongue, and people, and nation; And hast made us unto our God kings and priests: and we shall reign on the earth."* That is very clear.

DR. LINDSTED: As we look at chapters two and three of Revelation, we see a beautiful picture of the Church Age. In these chapters we read of seven Churches. These Churches represent different phases in the Church Age. The Church at Ephesus represented the first part of the Chruch Age. The Church of Smyrna represented the next phase of the Church Age; and so on down the line until we come to the Church at Laodicea; the end-time Church.

DR. GAVERLUK: The Church at Philadelphia escapes the Tribulation but the Church at Laodicea goes into the Tribulation. What we mean by that is simply that the unsaved go into the Tribulation because they are the ones represented by the Laodicean Church.

DR. LINDSTED: That is right. The Laodicean Church was spewed out of God's mouth. He would not spew out those who were Christians. Another thing I noticed, the Church at Philadelphia is a small Church. A Church without much strength compared to the forces around it. That is the picture of the true Christian today. Though they are small and have little strength, they have kept his word; they have not denied the name of Christ and he says: *"therefore I will keep thee from the hour of temptation . . . "*

In Revelation 2:7 we find the phrase: *"He that hath an ear, let him hear what the Spirit saith unto the churches . . . "* That phrase is repeated for each message to the seven churches. I believe at the close of chapter three and the beginning of chapter four, we find the rapture of the Church. It is interesting that as we go to Revelation 13:9 we find a similar phrase: *"If any man have an ear, let him hear."* Notice there is a difference between the phrase used in chapter 13 and the one used in chapters two and three. In chapters two and three it says: *" . . . let him hear what the Spirit saith unto the churches . . . "* In chapter 13, however, the Church is not mentioned because it is gone; it is no longer on the earth. So the book of Revelation even changes the language; even changes the warning. In chapters two and three, which represent the Church Age, the Church is addressed; but in chapter 13 we read of a general warning to any man living in that day.

DR. GAVERLUK: So in the book of Revelation, we do not see the Church after chapter four. Where does the Church go?

DR. LINDSTED: I am convinced the Church goes into the presence of God; into heaven. In chapter three of Revelation, we read of the Church Age. As it comes to an end, John is given an invitation by a voice, a trump of God, to *"come up hither."* As he goes, he sees a permanent throne that is set up. All the other thrones of the earth have been temporary, this one is permanent. Next he sees 24 other thrones with the elders seated on them. Notice the elders are clothed in white; they are sitting on thrones; and they have gold crowns. According to chapter five, verse six, Christ is in the midst of them. What a beautiful description that is of the Church.

As we come to chapter four, these 24 elders see God sitting on His throne and they begin to worship Him. From verse eight to the end of the chapter we read their praises to Him. *" . . . Holy, holy, holy, Lord God Almighty, which was, and is, and is to come. And when those beasts give glory and honor and thanks to him that sat on the throne, who liveth for ever and ever, The four and twenty elders fall down before him that sat on the throne, and worship him that liveth for ever and ever, and cast their crowns before the throne, saying, Thou are worthy, O Lord, to receive glory and honor and power . . . "*

As we go on to chapter five, we see God holding in His right hand, a book. This book is sealed with seven seals; I believe it is the title deeds of the earth. John begins to weep, because no one can be found who is worthy to open the book. Then an elder says to him in verse five: *" . . . Weep not: behold, the Lion of the tribe of Judah, the Root of David, hath prevailed to open the book, and to loose the seven seals thereof."* In verse six, John sees the one who is worthy, and He is a Lamb as it had been slain. This Lamb is of course, Christ, the Lamb of God who has been resurrected. All of heaven sees that He is worthy to take the book. In verse nine the heavens begin to sing a new song: *"Thou art worthy to take the book, and to open the seals thereof: for thou wast slain, and hast redeemed us to God by the blood out of every kindred, and tongue, and people, and nation."* In verse 12 the singing continues: *"Saying with a loud voice, Worthy is the Lamb that was slain to receive power, and riches, and wisdom, and strength, and honor, and Glory, and blessing."*

In chapter six, the Lamb takes the book and opens one of the seven seals. When He does this, out will come the Antichrist (chapter six verse two). Then He will open another seal and out will come war (chapter six verse three). This continues until all of the seals are opened. What I want to look at is not the seals that have been opened, but the time frame that is involved. The first seal, which is the seal that releases the Antichrist, cannot be opened until the book has been taken by the Lamb. Before the book can be taken, all of heaven must bow down and throw their crowns at the feet of the Lamb. Before the crowns can be thrown at the feet of Christ, the Church must be given crowns. The Church cannot receive its crowns before it has been raptured. Therefore, the Church must be raptured, taken out, before the Tribulation time occurs.

DR. GAVERLUK: That is a magnificent picture. It is simply breathtaking to try to understand. The events that we, the Church, are going to experience are so wonderful that they go beyond our comprehension. Those of us who have studied this for years, still feel that we do not grasp the full significance of these amazing things which are going to occur to us.

The promise for the future, the only guarantee we have for the future, is in a personal relationship with the Lord, Jesus Christ. This is God himself, who has come to planet Earth to die in our place; to take care of our own personal deaths. Then to raise us from the dead if we die before He comes. If we are alive when He comes, we are going to be a part of the rapture; we are gong to be snatched up; caught up to meet Him in the air. That is a moment to be desired by everyone.

It is simple to believe Jesus and accept Him as your personal savior. All you have to do is say a simple prayer like this: *"Lord Jesus, I believe you; I trust you; I love you; I want to serve you for the rest of my life. Forgive me of my sins."* A simple prayer like that and you pass from death to life because you have put your faith and trust in the Lord, Jesus Christ. If you have never done this, won't you please do it now, while there is still time?